BUSINESS RESEARCH AND REPORT WRITING

ROBERT L. SHURTER, PH.D.

Professor of English, Case Institute of Technology

J. PETER WILLIAMSON, LL.B., D.B.A.

Associate Professor of Law, University of Toronto
Visiting Associate Professor of Business Administration
Amos Tuck School of Business Administration, Dartmouth College

WAYNE G. BROEHL, JR., D.B.A.

Professor of Business Administration
Amos Tuck School of Business Administration, Dartmouth College

McGRAW-HILL BOOK COMPANY

New York   St. Louis   San Francisco   Toronto   London

BUSINESS RESEARCH AND REPORT WRITING

Business Research and Report Writing

Library of Congress Catalog Card Number 64–7737

07–057329–8

1314151617 MUMU 98

CONTENTS

INTRODUCTION

Reports in business are a part of the whole scheme of business communication. Much of the world's business would end tomorrow if we paid more than lip service to the maxims we have inherited on the subject of communication. At one time or another, we have all glibly repeated such old saws as "Silence is golden," "No news is good news," "What you don't know won't hurt you," and have expressed admiration for small boys who are "seen and not heard," perhaps because they will grow up to be "the strong, silent men" considered heroic in certain types of fiction.

These half-truths of our folklore are nonsense in today's complex, specialized business community, where a continuous exchange of ideas and information is an absolute necessity. "The first executive function," says Chester I. Barnard in his definitive book *The Functions of the Executive,* "is to develop and maintain a system of communication." [1] In the same vein, the editors of *Fortune* commented, "If business has a new motto, 'Communicate or Founder' would seem to be it." [2]

These comments should suffice to show the importance of communication skills in business. What do we mean by "communication"? We can define it quite simply as *imparting or exchanging thoughts or information*—and since we will be dealing with only one form of communication, we must add *in writing*. But such a definition really doesn't help very much. We can get closer to the fundamentals of written communication by thinking of it as a process which always includes:

1. A writer.
2. The material—facts, ideas, information, recommendations, conclusions—which he wants to communicate.
3. A reader. For certain forms of business communication we would be more realistic to say "a group of readers."

This analysis may be oversimplified, but it is better than the abstractions of our first definition because it puts human beings—a writer and reader(s)—into the act of communication. "It takes two to speak the truth," said Thoreau, "—one to speak and another to hear."

[1] Reprinted by permission of the Harvard University Press.

[2] Reprinted by special permission from *Fortune's* Communication Series, *Is Anybody Listening?* copyright 1950, by Time, Inc.

But in this two-person situation let there be no doubt about who bears the responsibility for effective communication. The responsibility rests on you as the writer. You might as well accept this responsibility right now. It will be forced on you in business. You will have to abandon certain alibis you may have used in the past. You won't be able to blame misunderstandings on "a stupid reader"; you'll have to make every effort to write with such clarity and simplicity that he can understand. You can't say that he is stubborn or pigheaded or narrow-minded because he doesn't agree with you; you'll have to use tact and persuasion and evidence to make him see your point of view. Of course, you may still fail to get your ideas across; it would be unrealistic to think that you can always succeed with your reader. But if you fail, you have at least done so with the knowledge that you did your best—and that is the essence of responsibility in writing, as in anything else.

Fulfilling your responsibility requires that you *think*. Think *before* you write, *when* you write—and then think about how you can improve or revise *after* you have written. Writing which serves your particular purpose requires that you think the purpose through. Clear writing stems from thoughtful planning. Concise writing results from thinking your way through to essentials, eliminating the extraneous and irrelevant. And writing which is correct and appropriate in style reveals that you have thought of how the reader will react and have designed your communication to produce the reactions you want.

We can sum up these observations on thinking, and at the same time state a major theme of this book, by saying that you must have your reader always in mind. You must always be thinking of what *he* wants to learn, what you want *him* to learn, what reactions you want to produce in *him* and what you want to avoid, and how your writing can accomplish this.

The more you can learn about orderly habits of thought and the logical sequence of events and ideas, the better you can organize your material. The more you can learn about psychology and human relations and people, the more you can know about your readers. These habits of thought and a broad knowledge of people are the most useful background you can have for writing in business. They will enable you to avoid the pitfalls of "thought-less" writing and accomplish the particular purposes you have in mind for a communication. You will, of course, have to supplement this background with a knowledge of the techniques of writing which are discussed in this book as they apply to the specific problems of writing reports.

If you are engaging in a career in business or industry, six words —or their equivalent—are an inevitable part of your future: "Give me a report on that." The report has become an essential means of business communication; even the facetious statement "It takes a ton of paper to produce a ton of product in today's business" is an acknowledgment of the importance of reports. Said Charles E. Wilson before a congressional committee: "No physical activity goes on in our modern age without a piece of paper going along to guide it."

Probably the best way to define a report is in terms of what it *does*. Its purpose, generally, is to provide managers with information on the basis of which they can decide or act. Professor C. A. Brown, chairman of the English Department of the General Motors Institute, defined a report in this way:

> We say it as simply as we possibly can, and that is, that a report is a communication from someone who has information to someone who wants to use that information. The report may be elaborately formal, it may be a letter, or in a great many organizations it is simply a memorandum, but it is always planned for use.

The usefulness of your reports is what you must constantly keep in mind. Whether a report is good or bad generally boils down to how useful it is to its readers. Suppose the sales manager of a manufacturing company is considering adding a new product to his line. He wants to know how well it would sell and how it should be priced. He asks his salesmen, or perhaps a market research staff, for reports that will help him answer these questions. He needs to know the cost of production and whether the company has the necessary manufacturing facilities. He asks production people for reports which answer these questions. The decision whether to manufacture and sell the product will be based on the reports. When production begins, reports will tell the sales and production managers whether the costs are within the expectations and whether the quantity and quality are satisfactory. Reports will tell the sales manager whether sales are up to expectations, whether competition has appeared unexpectedly, whether anticipated prices can be maintained. On the basis of these later reports, plans may be changed, new research undertaken, or production or sales methods changed. A great many reports will have been written, probably by many people. Each report will have had a specific purpose or set of purposes to serve; each will have been expected to enable its readers to do or to decide something. Whether or not a particular report was successful will have depended largely on how well the writer understood the use his readers expected to make of it.

An understanding of purpose is a good starting point in any report, and the following chapter is devoted to this topic. Chapters 2, 3, and 4 deal with problems of written expression, and Chapters 5 through 10 discuss specific aspects of reports.

1
THE PURPOSE
OF A REPORT

Before you can begin to plan the "how" of business writing, you have to understand the "why." Until you have established just what purposes a written communication is to serve—both your own and your readers' purposes—you cannot decide what is the most appropriate form of presentation. The failure of writers to think through their purposes probably causes more frustration to readers than any other writing fault. Here are a few examples taken from business and government:

A senior officer in the Federal government complained that all the reports written for him were five or six times as long as he thought they should be, vague, and hard to read. It turned out that the men writing these reports simply did not know exactly what purposes the reports were to serve. Consequently, they tried to serve every possible purpose, writing long and largely irrelevant reports.

A senior partner in a management consulting firm was considering a training program to improve the writing of the firm's engineers. The reports these men were writing to the firm's clients were eliciting a lukewarm response, yet the partner knew his men were highly competent engineers. A little investigation revealed that the engineers were accustomed to writing a routine report describing the work they had done and the recommendations they had come up with. It had never occurred to them that their readers were unlikely to adopt a recommendation that involved changing methods of operating a business unless they were shown clearly and emphatically what they had to gain by change. A client who was not "sold" on the consultant's recommendations rarely adopted them, and the reputation of the consulting firm suffered. The engineers had simply never been aware that one of the purposes of their reports was to "sell" the client on their recommendations.

A production manager was dissatisfied with the reports of an assistant, a recent graduate of a business school. The assistant had been asked to write a series of reports on the advisability of acquiring various kinds of new production equipment. The production manager intended to use these reports to justify to the top management his recommendations that the equipment be purchased. He felt the reports did a poor job of persuasion. It turned out that the assistant was not aware that the manager had already decided to recommend the purchases. He had assumed his reports were to serve as a basis for the manager's decisions; consequently, he had tried to present an objective and balanced analysis of the pros and cons.

In all three of these cases a writer was making an unsatisfactory impression simply because he did not understand the purpose of his writing. Time and time again, businessmen complain that the reports they receive do not tell them what they need to be told. Sometimes the fault lies with the reader himself: He either has given misleading instructions or has simply failed to indicate what purpose he expects the report to serve. Generally, however, it is the writer's fault. If he did not receive clear enough instructions, he should have gone back for more. Before he began work on his report, he should have been absolutely clear about what the reader expected from it.

Recommendation

Your reader may be expecting you to make a specific recommendation for a course of action. Let us take a situation where a company's sales manager has asked you for a report making a recommendation on whether or not to cut the price of a product. The sales manager, first of all, wants a specific recommendation. You must come up with a yes-or-no answer, and presumably, if you come up with a yes answer, you must indicate the specific amount by which the price should be reduced.

This is only a beginning, however. What sort of reasoning or justification of your conclusion does the sales manager expect you to give? If you are experienced in your job and he trusts your judgment, it may be that he will not expect much justification. On the other hand, if you are relatively inexperienced, and particularly if the sales manager has not yet begun to rely on you, he may require considerable justification of your conclusion. Even if you are experienced and the sales manager trusts your judgment, he may still want detailed reasoning and justification. He may be passing on your recommendation, and your reasons for it, to a higher official of the company. Or he may know that if the decision turns out to be a poor one, he will be asked to produce the reasoning that led to it. Hence he may want you to provide him now with your reasoning. And you, for your own purposes, may wish to have on record the reasons for your conclusion, in case it is criticized or reviewed later.

Suppose you have determined, then, that the sales manager wants not only your conclusion but your reasoning. It may still be important to know just why. If he is not prepared to accept your recommendation without your reasoning, then he probably wants the reasoning included in the main body of the report. If he wants your reasoning only as justification in case the decision is later criticized, then he may expect you to present the reasoning as a sort of appendix or attachment to your report. Before you can decide exactly what kind of report the sales manager expects, you will have to decide not only whether he wants your reasoning, but, if he does want it, why he wants it and in what form he wants it presented.

The reader of a report may, however, not be expecting a recommendation at all. He may be expecting you to present alternative courses of action, in a report containing the significant data and reasoning which might lead to a choice, but leaving it up to him to make the final decision. It is important to know whether the reader expects you to make the decision or expects you to leave this to him. It is frustrating to a reader who expected a concrete recommendation to find only a series of possibilities, with the choice or decision left to him.

If your report is to serve as the basis for someone else's decision, then you are going to have to include a good deal of data and reasoning. Just how much you should include will depend on whether your reader expects you to work with the data and reduce the choice to a simple weighing of pros and cons or whether he wants to go through the data himself. The more precisely you can pin such factors down, the better your report will serve its reader's needs. If he wants a concise presentation of the major factors, he will not be pleased with a lengthy report that presents only masses of raw data. On the other hand, if he likes to work with raw data and draw his own conclusions, he will not be pleased with a concise summary of the significant factors and no mention of the data that went into it.

Information

Your reader may simply ask for information, a deceptively simple request. Why does he want the information? This is a crucial question because the amount of information which you present, and the form in which you present it, must be tied to the use that is to be made of it.

Suppose, for example, that the same sales manager asks for sales information on a particular product. He may want the information in order to decide whether the price should be cut and, if so, by how much. He may want the information in order to project future sales for the product and so establish production schedules or inventory levels. He may want the information in order to pass it on to a superior who is endeavoring to establish the profitability of various company products. Obviously, the kinds of information wanted and the way in which the information should be presented are not the same for each of these purposes. If you work on the assumption that the sales manager wants your information in order to plan inventory levels, and it turns out that he really wanted it in order to determine whether the product is profitable, he is likely to be dissatisfied with your report.

Demonstrating Your Ability

Your reader may be quite frankly asking for an indication of your own ability when he asks for a report. This is particularly true when he asks you for a progress report. What he is looking for is evidence of what you have accomplished. It may even be that he is asking for a progress report which he will pass on to his superior as evidence of what he and his staff are accomplishing. In the first case, you will be demonstrating your own ability and accomplishment to your immediate superior; in the second case, you are enabling him to demonstrate his abilities and accomplishments to his superior and indirectly displaying your own abilities.

Demonstrating ability is especially important for a young and inexperienced writer who has not yet earned the confidence and respect of his business organization. It may not seem to you very important to convince others in business that you are able to write well. But your writing conveys more than your ability to write well. It demonstrates your ability to think, to analyze, and to make sound judgments. Most people react unfavorably to a badly written report, but relatively few are able to tell exactly what is wrong with it. If you write an inadequate report, your readers are just as likely to blame you for poor thinking as for poor writing. In fact, there is a very common belief that bad writing *always* results from bad thinking. Ineffective writing, then, can gain you a reputation for illogical thinking and bad judgment. The fact that this conclusion may be unjustified will be small consolation to you.

What you write in business may well go to people with whom you have no other contact. This provides both an opportunity and a risk. Your letters, memorandums, or reports may be passed on by a superior to people further up the line; because of this, you may be able to demonstrate your ability to people who are in a position to affect your promotions and the kind of work assigned to you but who are generally inaccessible to you. Even the routine writing you do for an immediate superior may be handed on to other people without your expecting it. This means that a piece of work hastily or carelessly done, which you did not expect to go beyond the man with whom you are already on pretty good terms, may actually reach some influential people who have no other knowledge of you. The result inevitably is that they form a low opinion of your ability.

It is obvious to a college student that the principal purpose of his written work is to demonstrate his knowledge and ability to an instructor. Yet many people forget this purpose when they start writing reports, letters, or memorandums in business. You cannot afford to forget how important your writing is to your personal success.

If you remember the personal importance of your writing, you will have made a good beginning. You will next have to identify the specific purposes you should be trying to serve in any particular writing situation. For example, you may be attempting to persuade someone to do something, providing information to help someone do or decide something, or trying to build goodwill for your company. It may surprise you that anyone could have trouble identifying purposes such as these, but recall the examples quoted at the beginning of this chapter. It is crucial to have the correct set of purposes in mind.

Here are a few questions that may help you to establish the purposes of a report. These questions may not always be appropriate and you may have to think of others yourself. They will, however, give you a start.

1. To whom am I addressing my report? Who else may read it?
2. If the report was requested by the reader, has he told me specifically what he wants? Should I ask for clarification? Are there any unstated purposes my reader probably wants the report to serve—purposes he is not likely to tell me about? If others may read the report, what purposes will they expect it to serve?
3. If I am writing not in response to a request but on my own initiative, do I know exactly what I am trying to accomplish? What do I want the reader to do? to say? to believe?
4. Am I trying to persuade my reader? Am I attempting to change or strengthen his convictions, or is he undecided? Am I sure what his convictions are? Do I know why he holds them?
5. How important will my report be to my reader? Will he be impatient with a long, detailed discussion? Will he think I have done a careless, skimpy job if I am brief?

2

CLARITY AND COHERENCE

Clarity is usually assumed to be essential to business communication.
Occasionally there may be good reason for being unclear. There is a story to the effect that the management of a British steamship company once decided that the officers of its passenger ships should wear swords. This, the management felt, would add to the glamor of a transatlantic crossing and appeal to the passengers. But because the wearing of swords might make company personnel resemble naval officers, the management decided to request permission of the British Admiralty before making the change. The Admiralty was not enthusiastic about the idea and yet did not wish to say no. Finally a reply was drafted, saying that the Admiralty had no objection to the company's proposal provided that the swords were worn "on the right side." This put the company in a dilemma. Did the letter mean the Admiralty insisted that swords be worn on the *correct* side, which is the left side, or were the company's officers to wear their swords on the *right-hand* side, to distinguish themselves from naval officers? Too embarrassed to ask for clarification, the management dropped the whole idea, and the Admiralty achieved a quiet triumph.

You will rarely run into a situation calling for lack of clarity. But it is important to think of clarity, or any other attribute of writing, as serving some purpose in a particular piece of writing, rather than as an end in itself.

Many elements of writing contribute to clarity, and we shall discuss two of them—correctness and style—in subsequent chapters. But probably the most important aspect of clarity is coherence. Coherence refers to connections between words, sentences, or paragraphs, or between topics or ideas. In a coherent presentation each sentence is connected in some logical way with both the preceding and the following sentences. Each topic or idea appears to follow logically from the preceding topic, and a reader is never led to expect a discussion of one topic only to find that the writer has chosen another.

You should regard every statement you make in a written communication, from the title onward, as involving a sort of contract with your reader in which you undertake to discuss certain topics and ideas. If the title of a report you write is "Company Policy in Hiring College Graduates," then you have promised your reader that this is what you will talk about, this and nothing else. If you deviate from this topic, your reader may quite properly be surprised and annoyed. But promises are made in almost every statement you write, not just in titles. If you begin a paragraph with the sentence "We have found several small colleges in the Midwest to be good sources for new employees," then you have led your reader to believe that you will go on to discuss the usefulness, as sources of employees, of small colleges in the Midwest, or at least the usefulness of small colleges generally. If you immediately switch to a discussion of what beginning salaries the company should offer in New York City, the reader is surprised and confused. Your writing is incoherent.

Coherence usually depends on good organization—arranging your topics and ideas in the proper sequence and linking them by logical transitions. The sequence is especially important in organizing sentences.

Organization of a Sentence

SCHOOL BOARD BANS SEX BEHIND CLOSED DOORS

You have probably seen statements similar to this newspaper headline. Their humor lies in the location of a modifying phrase—in this case "behind closed doors"—next to a noun it was never intended to modify. A reader tends to link in his mind ideas and words that are located together, so that although a little thought leads to the conclusion that the writer meant to refer to a closed school board meeting, the first impression is of something quite different.

Here is a more complex example:

(1) He is aware that he should uphold the authority to fire workers of his supervisors who disobey orders whenever possible as a management representative.

The sentence begins fairly well but soon degenerates into an incoherent scramble of thoughts. We will try to put the writer's meaning into coherent form. First we'll isolate the satisfactory beginning: "He is aware that he should uphold the authority to fire workers." This is coherent and expresses the main thought of the sentence. *Of his supervisors* is out of place because it appears to refer to *workers* although it seems clear that the writer intended it to refer to *authority*. Otherwise there would be nothing to tell us whose authority he is talking about. So we move *of his supervisors* up to follow *authority*. Now we have:

> He is aware that he should uphold the authority of his supervisors to fire workers who disobey orders whenever possible as a management representative.

This is better: *who disobey orders* has now fallen in place after *workers,* the word to which it was evidently intended to refer, instead of seeming to refer to *supervisors*.

But *whenever possible* and *as a management representative* still seem wrongly placed. *As a management representative* seems at first glance to refer to *workers* but it can really refer only to *he;* there is no other single person mentioned in the sentence. To make the reference quite clear, we could shift this phrase to precede or follow *he*. The expression "He, as a management representative, is aware" is correct but a little awkward, especially as the beginning of a rather long and involved sentence. "As a management representative, he is aware" is better.

We now have to decide what to do with *whenever possible*. There is genuine doubt here as to what the writer meant. Did he really mean to refer to workers who disobey orders whenever possible? Probably not, because this would limit the application of the whole sentence to an insignificant number of situations. There are only three verbs in the sentence to which *whenever possible* could refer. If it doesn't refer to *disobey,* then it can refer only to *should uphold* or to *to fire*. Probably the writer intended it to refer to *should uphold*. On this assumption we rewrite the sentence as follows:

> As a management representative, he is aware that he should uphold whenever possible the authority of his supervisors to fire workers who disobey orders.

What we have done is to reconstruct the sentence so that the apparent references—apparent because of their location—are the correct ones. The reader is no longer temporarily or even permanently confused by apparent references that the writer never intended.

Emphasis

An important element of clarity is proper emphasis. This means simply that important ideas should be emphasized, less important ones subordinated. In a paragraph or a report, position may indicate importance. A topic sentence, at the beginning of the paragraph, may introduce the central idea. Or, the paragraph may lead up to the important topic, which is given an emphatic position at the end. In a report, the same rule holds true. Central ideas or recommendations should not be buried in the text, but should be given an eye-catching place at the beginning or the end.

The way of achieving proper emphasis on the sentence level is slightly different. The general rule is that the important point should be in the main, or independent, clause. As an example, let us look at the sentence we rewrote in the previous section:

> As a management representative, he is aware that he should uphold whenever possible the authority of his supervisors to fire workers who disobey orders.

As this sentence stands, its dominant idea is *he is aware.* If we want the reader to be struck by the importance of *a management representative should uphold the authority of his supervisors,* we will have to remove this thought from its subordinate position. If we consider awareness equally important to our message, we will have to construct our sentence with two independent clauses, separated by a semicolon:

> A management representative should, whenever possible, uphold the authority of his supervisors to fire workers who disobey orders; he is aware of this.

Parallel Constructions

A useful device for achieving clarity, and one that most of us use frequently, if not always correctly, is parallel construction. A great many specific purposes may be served by parallel constructions, but generally these purposes involve some sort of comparison. Two or more statements present ideas that contain similarities or contrasts, and the writer uses a parallel construction to emphasize these similarities and contrasts and to make them clear.

Here is a simple example:

(2) The law of supply and demand is related to the well-known fact that as the price of goods rises the demand for them declines.

The parallel construction lies in the statements "as the price of goods rises" and "the demand for them declines." The first uses the words *price* and *rises* and the second uses the words to be compared to them: *demand* and *declines*. *Rises* and *declines* are opposites, and the construction is meant to emphasize the opposite behavior of two things. The two things themselves are not opposites; they are merely different, but they behave in opposite ways.

Here is a less obvious example:

(3) The management of the company can choose either to raise its scale of starting salaries and thereby attract better qualified college graduates, or to save its money and be satisfied with less qualified new employees.

The "either . . . or" construction is a parallel construction. The writer is describing two different courses of action (not necessarily opposite, but different), and he wants to make this difference, and the differing consequences, clear.

At this point you may wonder what is so special about a parallel construction. The answer lies in the frequency with which the effectiveness of this construction is destroyed by mistakes.

Statements that the writer intends to form into a parallel construction must be *grammatically* parallel. Consider the following example:

(4) The company's high-quality products, reasonable prices, good service, and in general, running respectable stores, have given it a good reputation.

The writer has set out to tell us that four features of the company have given it a good reputation. He has put the four into what looks like a parallel construction, but he has been careless about his grammar and word choice. Nouns can be used in parallel with nouns, as: "high-quality products, reasonable prices, good service." And gerunds can be used in parallel with gerunds: *offering* high-quality products, *selling* at reasonable prices, *maintaining* good service, *running* respectable stores. But this mixture of the two—high-quality products, reasonable prices, good service, running respectable stores—is ineffective. The reader sees products, prices, and service as three things the company offers, or maintains, or does something with or to. He sees running stores not as something the company does something *with* but as something the company *does*. His mind easily groups, compares, adds up, or contrasts the things that the company does something *with,* and it deals equally easily with things the company *does,* but he has trouble handling a mixture of the two. In more technical terms, we can say the parallel construction depends, for its effect, on its symmetry. The things to be compared, contrasted, or added up should be easily identified by their grammatical form. What can you do to correct example (4)? You could write:

> The company's offering high-quality products, reasonable prices, good service, and in general, running respectable stores, has given it a good reputation.

The parallel now is between *offering* and *running,* both things the company *does* (and both gerunds, in grammatical terms). A better, because less awkward, version is probably:

> The company's high-quality products, reasonable prices, good service, and policy of running respectable stores have given it a good reputation.

The parallel is now among *products, prices, service,* and *policy,* all nouns, all things the company does something *with* or *to.*

We turn now from grammatical aspects of parallel construction to the matter of precision in identifying the things to be paralleled. You must be sure your parallel constructions emphasize the comparisons you want. Can you find the false parallel in the following?

(5) The cost advantages enjoyed by foreign producers are off-set to some extent by the better reputations of United States manufacturers.

The writer intended to contrast the cost advantages of foreign companies with the better reputations of domestic companies. But his natural tendency to avoid the monotony of using the same word too often led him to describe the foreign companies as foreign *producers* and the domestic companies as *manufacturers*. His intended sharp contrast between *foreign* and *United States* manufacturers is blurred by the suggestion that he is also contrasting characteristics of *producers* and *manufacturers*.

Here is another example. The writer is describing two kinds of producers of bicycles: manufacturers, who make all their parts and then assemble them; and assemblers, who buy all their parts from manufacturers and assemble them. Both produce the same finished product.

(6) The cost advantages enjoyed by foreign manufacturers of bicycles are to some extent offset by the better reputation of United States assemblers.

A reader simply doesn't know whether the contrast the writer intended was between foreign cost advantages and domestic reputations, or between manufacturers' cost advantages and assemblers' reputations, or some combination of both.

We will conclude this section by putting together a parallel construction. This will involve taking the ideas expressed in a sentence that does not include a parallel construction and stating them more effectively in parallel form. The example is from a review of an accounting book.

(7) This book makes a good text for college students, and businessmen will find it even more useful for enlarging their knowledge of accounting.

First we have to decide exactly what the writer means. He says the book is a good text for college students. This seems clear enough. But his statement that businessmen will find it "more useful" is ambiguous. More useful than what? Does he mean that businessmen will find it more useful than something else for learning about accounting, or that they will find it more useful for learning about accounting than for something else, or that businessmen will get more out of the book than college students? It seems probable that this last meaning is what the writer intended.

We want a construction, then, that points out that the book is a good text for college students and is even better, used in a different way, for businessmen. We can now begin to see the parallel statements as something like: good, as a text, for college students; better, as a means of enlarging their knowledge of accounting, for businessmen. We might then rewrite the example as:

> This book is good, as a text, for college students, and even better, as a means of enlarging their knowledge of accounting, for businessmen.

This can stand some improvement, but we have the basic elements of the parallel construction worked out. It may occur to you that since a contrast is being drawn, the word *but* may be more effective than *and* in linking the parallel statements, and you may be able to smooth out the two statements and remove some of the commas. The following is suggested:

> This book will be useful as a college text, but even more valuable to the businessman, as a means of enlarging his knowledge of accounting.

Organization of Paragraphs

Paragraphs, like sentences, demand carefully arranged sequences of topics and ideas. But paragraph construction makes two demands that rarely concern you in building sentences. A paragraph must be built around a single theme or major topic, and the ideas or minor topics that are discussed in the paragraph must be connected with each other by logical transitions.[1] A sentence is usually short enough that every part deals with a single topic or theme, and you rarely find so many ideas in a sentence that it is difficult to connect them.

[1] Transitions between paragraphs are discussed in Chapters 7 and 8.

Most writing texts will tell you that a paragraph should deal with a *single topic*. This is fine as long as you know what a single topic is. Probably the best test to use is this: Put yourself in your reader's place, read over your paragraph and decide whether there is a central theme or major topic that runs through the entire paragraph. If there is not *some* such theme or topic, then you do not have a satisfactory paragraph. Either it should be broken into two or more paragraphs or it should be rewritten.

The first sentence of your paragraph should indicate the major topic of that paragraph. You may use a *topic sentence,* one that states the topic explicitly, or you may merely imply in your first sentence what your major topic is. In any case, your reader is going to decide on the basis of this sentence what *he* thinks the major topic is, and he will expect you to stick to that topic. It is this consistency that is called *unity* in a paragraph.

Unity requires that the minor topics of your paragraph—what you have to say about the major topic—all be part of the major topic or be closely related to it. To achieve this unity, once you have selected your minor topics, you must establish a logical sequence for them, as in the construction of sentences, and once the sequence is established, you must devise transitions to carry the reader's attention from one minor topic to the next in what appears to him a logical way.

We will turn now to some examples illustrating the importance of unity and how to achieve it by the selection of minor topics within a paragraph. At the same time we will deal with the logical sequence of these topics. Following this will be a discussion of transitions among the topics.

Unity and Logical Sequence

The following excerpts are from a report written to three young men planning to open a repertory theater. They had very little business experience and turned to a businessman for advice. His report began:

(8) I think that the idea of forming an experimental repertory theater is excellent. However, you should consider starting the project on a smaller scale.

This seems to be a good beginning. The writer has come directly to the point and offers a specific recommendation. What do you expect will follow these two sentences? Probably a discussion of why or how the theater should be started on a smaller scale. Small-scale operation seems to be the major topic of the paragraph. Here is how the report actually progressed:

(9) I think that the idea of forming an experimental repertory theater is excellent. However, you should consider starting the project on a smaller scale. The statement of the general manager of a similar venture attributed its failure to inexperienced management.

The third sentence, instead of dealing with small scale, has switched to inexperience. Is there any connection between the first two sentences and the third? Perhaps, but the writer certainly hasn't told us what it is. We are left wondering whether the topic of small-scale operations has been abandoned and why inexperience has been introduced. Now we add the writer's fourth and fifth sentences:

(10) I think that the idea of forming an experimental repertory theater is excellent. However, you should consider starting the project on a smaller scale. The statement of the general manager of a similar venture attributed its failure to inexperienced management. The man who is to be your business manager has not the experience to operate such a large enterprise as you are planning. Besides, the rest of the group have had little theatrical experience and are not well known.

At last we know why inexperience was brought in. The writer apparently believes this group has the experience necessary to run a small operation (at least he implies this), but not a large one. But we had to read through one distracting and apparently irrelevant sentence to find this out. And even now we are not sure why that third sentence was included. Was it intended to prove that inexperience dooms a large venture but not a small one? It certainly doesn't say so. It simply tells us that the failure of another venture, which may have been large or small, has been attributed to inexperience.

The fifth sentence, too, has added a new topic. The writer says the members of the group are not well known. Is this intended to strengthen the argument for small-scale operations? Probably, but the writer doesn't tell us why. He seems to have dragged in another topic that may or may not be relevant. He certainly doesn't show why it is relevant.

His next two sentences, still in the same paragraph, were the following:

(11) You intend to invest $20,000 to rebuild an old factory building in a city populated by people you regard as "Philistines." As your repertoire will be experimental theater, how can you appeal to this group of people?

What has happened to the theme of small-scale operation? It seems to have been dropped completely when the writer switched to the "Philistines." He gives us no explanation for the switch, and in fact he seems to be arguing against any theatrical venture, large or small. Probably what he intended to say was that a very small part of the city's population would patronize the proposed theater and hence it should be kept small. But he didn't say this.

We might rewrite the entire paragraph as follows, keeping to the theme of optimism but small-scale operation, which is what the writer presumably had in mind.

I think that the idea of forming an experimental repertory theater is excellent. However, you should consider starting the project on a smaller scale. Your business manager does not have the experience necessary to operate the large enterprise you are planning, and the rest of the group is inexperienced as well. Lack of experience has been blamed for the failure of a venture similar to yours. Another reason for small-scale operation is the probability that only a small segment of the city's population will be interested in experimental theater. You yourselves characterize this population as "Philistine."

Notice that we have preserved the theme, or major topic, throughout the paragraph. And we have arranged the sequence of ideas so that each one seems to follow logically from the one before.

All of this may seem picayune to you. A common reaction of a sloppy writer to a reader's complaint is: "But you know what I mean." And in fact we were able to deduce what the writer probably had in mind even when he seemed to be wandering hopelessly. But your job as a writer in business is not to provide guessing games for your reader. Let him know very quickly when you begin a paragraph what that paragraph is about. And then stick to your topic. Make sure not only that each sentence is related to your topic, but also that this is obvious to your reader. The writer of the paragraph we have been discussing may have known perfectly well why a "Philistine" population indicated a small theater. But he didn't bother to show us why, and we had to puzzle it out.

At least we were able to puzzle out that paragraph and reconstruct it in coherent form. But can you do the same for the next three paragraphs in the report?

(12) The general idea of your project is to fuse the American and English traditions in a repertory theater. Therefore my suggestion is the following:

We know about a successful repertory theater established seven years ago in your city operating in a tiny building.

As you want to stay in the city I suggest you rent a small place there.

What do you expect after reading the first of these three paragraphs (12)? Surely a suggestion as to how the three men may accomplish their objective of fusing the American and English theater traditions. But what actually comes next is a statement about another theater operating in a very small building. Is there any logical connection at all? There doesn't seem to be. The writer has apparently returned to the theme of small-scale operations, pointing out that another repertory theater is successfully operating on a small scale, and concluding that this group should rent a small place too.

The first of the three paragraphs in (12) is simply incomprehensible as it stands. The author may have believed it to be relevant, but there is simply no clue from which we could deduce the relevance. This is writing at its most incoherent. You can probably see why a reader of this report might conclude that the writer just couldn't think clearly.

Transitions

Transitions are what make a paragraph "hang together." You can think of transitions in two senses: as *logical connections* among ideas or as *mechanical aids* in linking these ideas. Consider the example:

(13) We do not have the experience necessary to operate a large theater; we shall have to be content with a small one.

There is a logical connection between the topics of lack of experience and limitation to only small-scale operations. One is the cause of the other. We can add a mechanical transition—the word *therefore*—to obtain the following:

(14) We do not have the experience necessary to operate a large theater; therefore, we shall have to be content with a small one.

We have actually discussed logical connections already, as part of the arrangement of topics in a logical sequence. In this section we shall be concerned with mechanical transitions.

Mechanical transitions may be words, phrases, clauses, or whole sentences. Typical transition words are *and, but, also, therefore, however, since, moreover, first, next, finally*. Transition phrases that are often useful are *in addition, at the same time, as well*. None of these expressions is new to you, nor is the idea of mechanical transitions. In fact, the subject is important because of the common overuse and misuse of transitions, not because of widespread failure to use them. To begin with, if your sequence of topics is not logical, so that you are placing topics with no logical connection next to each other, no mechanical transition will create a connection that seems reasonable to your reader. And, even if there is a logical connection among your topics, you may find yourself using the wrong transitions or using transitions where none are needed.

Consider the following example. It comes from a letter sent to its customers by an investment banking firm:

(15) Net long-term capital gains are taxable at a maximum effective rate of 25%. That is, only half of the net long-term gain is added to ordinary income in computing the tax.

Even if you are not familiar with the taxation of long-term capital gains under the Internal Revenue Code, you should be able to see that something is wrong here. If you are familiar with the tax rules, you know that there are two significant aspects to the taxation of long-term capital gains: Only half the gain is added to ordinary income in computing income tax, and the effective rate on the gain is limited to 25 per cent. These two aspects are not the same or even interdependent. They are logically related only because together they account for the special way in which long-term capital gains are taxed. The example above uses what we might call a false transition. The writer has used *that is* to provide a mechanical connection between his two topics, implying that the second somehow explains the first. There is no such logical relationship here. Only a conjunction which does not connote dependence—for example, *and, in addition* —can link the two ideas.

It is natural to prefer a transition implying logical connection to one that is simply a conjunction, such as *and*. And this is probably why you so often find expressions such as *that is* or *therefore* used to begin a paragraph that has no causal connection with the one that went before.

Transitions can be overdone. If a connection between two topics or ideas is perfectly clear to a reader, the addition of a transition will not contribute to his understanding and will probably slow him down and give an impression of childish writing. Compare the following two paragraphs. Do the transitions added in the second serve any purpose?

(16) A large-scale operation can be successful only if it is well-financed and the management is experienced. Your manager is not experienced, and you have little capital. You should limit yourselves to small-scale operation.

A large-scale operation can be successful only if it is well-financed and the management is experienced. But your manager is not experienced, and second, you have little capital. Therefore, you should limit yourselves to small-scale operations.

In the following example at least one transition is used in each sentence following the first. (The transitions are italicized.) Which do you think are useful in guiding a reader? Which are unnecessary because they only point out what is obvious? And which transitions are actually false, in that they imply logical connections which do not exist?

(17) I think that the idea of forming a repertory theater is excellent. *However,* you should consider starting the project on a smaller scale. *This is because* your business manager does not have the experience necessary to operate the large enterprise you are planning. *Therefore,* he is qualified to run only a small-scale operation. *Also,* lack of experience has been blamed for the failure of a venture similar to yours. *Another* reason for small-scale operation is the probability that only a small segment of the city's population will be interested in experimental theater. *This is because* you yourselves characterize this population as "Philistine."

However is useful in signaling a qualification to the statement made in the first sentence. Without it the second sentence may seem to contradict the first. *This is because* is probably superfluous, although it is not incorrect. *Therefore,* on the other hand, is probably incorrect. The fact that a man is not experienced enough to operate a large enterprise does not prove that he is qualified to run a small one. He may or may not be.

Also is not false (it does not imply a nonexistent logical relation), but it is temporarily misleading to a reader. He expects *also* to be followed by another reason for small-scale operation, but instead he is told why experience is important.

Another helps to bring the reader's mind back to reasons for small-scale operation after a brief digression to show why experience is important. You cannot avoid occasional digressions, and you may have to provide reminders of your principal topic.

This is because is false. The probability described in the preceding sentence is not caused by anyone's characterization. The writer's guess that certain things are probable is consistent with the reader's characterization, and this consistency may help convince the reader that the writer is correct, but there is no causal relationship involved.

Compare the example with the rewritten paragraph on page 27.

Word Choice

The English language is unusually rich in words whose meanings differ only slightly from those of other words. It is possible, in English, for a writer to express his ideas with a high degree of precision and to indicate very fine distinctions in meaning. On the other hand, it is especially easy for a writer with an incomplete understanding of the English language to confuse and mislead his readers with poorly chosen words.

Sometimes the poor choice stems simply from the writer's misunderstanding of a word's meaning. When the author of a current text on financial management wrote "There are several pragmatic reasons which mitigate against sharply drawn lines of demarcation," he confused *mitigate,* which means reduce the severity of, with *militate,* which means to have force or effect for or against. His mistake is perhaps less embarrassing than that of the consultant who wrote "This is an important decision and must be approached with levity," under the impression that *levity* meant seriousness, when in fact it means frivolity.

The obvious moral is: Know the meaning of a word before you use it. If you have any doubt, consult a dictionary. If you can't conveniently use a dictionary at the time you are writing, then use another word whose meaning you are sure of. Several texts contain lists of words most commonly misused, and you may find in them words whose meaning you have never understood. Some of these texts are referred to at the end of this chapter.

The wrong use of a word is certainly something to avoid. But a more common example of poor word choice involves the use of vague, general words instead of informative, precise ones. Jargon is a form of vagueness. Consider the word *finalize.* Some will object because it is a verb constructed by adding *ize* to an adjective. There is nothing wrong with this; this is how the language grows. The real fault in the word is the fact that it doesn't tell us anything. When a businessman says that he is going to *finalize* an advertisement this afternoon, he may mean that he is going to make a final decision on the content of the advertisement, or obtain someone else's final decision, or that he is going to complete the layout of the advertisement, or that he is going to place an order for the running of the advertisement, or that he is going to approve the running of the advertisement, or obtain someone else's approval, or probably any one of several other things that will complete some stage in the preparation and running of an advertisement. Instead of finding and using the term that describes precisely what he is going to do, he reaches for a vague word that gives a general idea of the kind of activity that will occupy him for the afternoon.

The use of the suffix -*wise* also leads to vague writing. When a businessman says, "Tax-wise, that would be a good course of action," does he mean the action will reduce taxes, postpone them, eliminate them, cause a shift from one form of tax to another, make it easier to pay the tax or to calculate it, or what? The real objection to jargon is that it does not fill any need. It does not convey a meaning that cannot be better conveyed by well-established words.

Some rather well-established words are also used frequently in business writing to convey only vague, general impressions. *Problem* is a favorite word of those who cannot be bothered to think of the right words to express their thoughts precisely. Here is an example:

(18) In trying to increase his company's efficiency, Mr. Withers faces the problems of union opposition, what to do with employees no longer needed, not knowing how much money is available for modernization, and that after he is all through his products may be obsolete.

Problems are something we *solve*. A union's opposition is not a problem; it is an obstacle, or perhaps a difficulty that we try to *overcome*. What to do with superfluous employees is a question, something that must be *answered*. Not knowing how much money is available is probably an obstacle or difficulty, and that the products may be obsolete is a risk that Mr. Withers must *run*. Here is a rewritten version of the sentence:

In trying to increase his company's efficiency, Mr. Withers faces the obstacle of union opposition and the difficulty of not knowing how much money is available for modernization; he must answer the question of what to do with employees no longer needed; and he runs the risk that after he is all through his products may be obsolete.

Phase is another word that is often used as a sort of fill-in when a writer can't think of the right word to express his meaning:

(19) All phases of the company are currently moving to a position of optimum efficiency, productivity, and organization.

A phase is an aspect of something whose appearance changes. A company can go through phases as its characteristics change. But here, presumably, what the writer had in mind were not different stages through which the company was moving but different parts of the company, perhaps divisions or departments. Exactly what he had in mind we don't know.

The word *area,* commonly used to describe a body of knowledge or a specialty, can be confusing when it is used in conjunction with a concept of space:

(20) In the area of plant location there is still a need for planning.

"The area of plant location" suggests a physical area reserved for the location of a plant, but the rest of the sentence indicates that this is not the kind of area that the writer had in mind. He is referring to the topic or job of plant location.

These examples indicate the need to examine your writing constantly to see if you are taking refuge in vague, general words when you should be finding precise words that tell your reader exactly what you mean instead of just giving him the general idea. It is very easy to slip into generalization. And it is very easy to read generalizations, but a reader who is looking for useful analysis or information will realize sooner or later that he is not finding it.

Word choice is a large topic and an important one. But beyond the advice given above, it is difficult to provide any useful guidance without discussing a great many individual words and ultimately writing an entire book on the subject. Several authors have done just that, and the following books are suggested as supplementary reading.

H. W. FOWLER, *A Dictionary of Modern English Usage,* Oxford: Clarendon Press, 1953.
This is a useful general reference on word usage.

WILLIAM GILMAN, *The Language of Science,* New York: Harcourt, Brace & World, Inc., 1961.
This book is designed for engineers, scientists, and those who are writing technical articles and reports.

SIR ERNEST GOWERS, *Plain Words: Their ABC,* New York: Alfred A. Knopf, Inc., 1954.
This book was originally written for the British civil service, to help eliminate the use of jargon in the writing of government officials. It is highly readable and especially useful to business writers.

J. B. GREENOUGH AND G. L. KITTREDGE, *Words and Their Ways in English Speech,* Boston: Beacon Press, 1962.
This is a book for students of literature, interesting and scholarly, less useful for business writing than some of the preceding.

3

WRITING CORRECTLY

Attitudes toward correctness in writing run the gamut. At one extreme is the famous comment of Will Rogers: "A lot of people who don't say 'ain't,' ain't eating." At the other are the well-known advertisements with a gentleman pointing an ominous finger and asking: "Do *you* make these mistakes in English—mistakes which can be ruinous to your career?" Between these two extremes we can probably find agreement that correctness is important to business writers if it is not extended to the slavish worship of rules that marks the pedant.

Correctness is important in achieving clarity. Incorrect writing is frequently ambiguous, sometimes quite misleading, and usually difficult to understand. This is not always true, of course. There is no lack of clarity in the statement: "I ain't got my pay yet today." You avoid this kind of writing not for the sake of clarity but because you don't want to be thought uneducated. And there is a third reason for writing correctly: to avoid annoying a reader who recognizes incorrect writing when he sees it and doesn't like it. (It is true that *ain't* has made an appearance in the controversial third edition of *Webster's New International Dictionary,* but try using it seriously in a business letter or report and see what the reaction is!)

There are sometimes good reasons for writing incorrectly in business, just as there are sometimes reasons for striving to be unclear. Writers of advertising copy, for example, will deliberately write incorrectly to achieve a folksy impression. And we have already referred to a desire to avoid pedantry. Most business writers will choose "It's me," in preference to "It's I," although the latter is technically the correct form. But the occasions for willfully flouting the rules for correct writing are few and far between, and we will devote no more time to them.

To write correctly, you have to know grammar. Many people believe they can write with a reasonable degree of correctness without a knowledge of grammar. And students, particularly, often argue that they can't learn grammar or that grammar is not important. It is true that some people write correctly by intuition, without a thorough knowledge of grammar, but they are exceptional. Most of us can write reasonably correctly most of the time by intuition, but if we don't know the rules, we will inevitably make mistakes without noticing them, we will be careless because we won't know what to watch for, and when we recognize incorrect writing, we won't know what to do about it because we won't really understand what is wrong. The person who knows the rules, the principles, of any activity—be it golf, chess, sharpening a chisel, organizing a membership drive, or writing—always performs more effectively because he knows not only *what* he is doing at each step, but *why* he is doing it. To argue that you can't learn grammar is nonsense. As the writer of a calculus text said, in a much-quoted encouragement to his students: "What one fool can do, another can." And plenty of fools have mastered correct writing. But learning grammar is work; we are not born with an innate sense of grammar any more than we are born with the ability to play a violin. And it is a kind of work that admittedly is not very popular.

But there are certain standards of usage you must know, not because the grammar handbooks say so, but *because you cannot be a competent writer without knowing them.* You can go too far in following rules. This is the mark of the purist, the office pest. He insists on observing rules that are becoming obsolete. Rules follow usage by what used to be called "cultivated people," not the other way around. About six hundred years ago Geoffrey Chaucer quite properly used triple negatives, as in "There was never no man nowhere so virtuous," but subsequent changes in usage have made this form of expression obsolete and ungrammatical. What you should aim at is the standard of best usage in business writing *today.*

This does not mean that grammar is a slippery thing that changes constantly and cannot be pinned down. There are many rules of grammar that are absolutely fixed and unchanging. Others are changing, but you must still determine what is considered correct today.

You can begin to bring yourself up to date by forgetting two "rules" that for some reason seem to be stamped indelibly in the mind of almost everyone who has taken courses in English. The first is that you should try *to never split* an infinitive. The second is nicely stated in the following bit of verse:

> The grammar has a rule absurd
> Which I would call an outworn myth:
> A preposition is a word
> You mustn't end a sentence with!

These "rules" have a purpose: to avoid the lack of emphasis in a sentence ending on a minor note, such as a preposition; and to avoid the awkwardness of putting unnecessary words between *to* and the verb form of the infinitive. But there are times when you'll find it less awkward to end with prepositions and to split infinitives. Said Sir Winston Churchill in an ironic comment on this overprissiness, "This is arrant pedantry up with which I will not put." The late Carl Van Doren, a great teacher and writer, used to tell a story to end all stories about prepositions. A father was asked by his small boy, who was sick in bed upstairs, to read from the boy's favorite book. He selected the wrong book and was greeted by, "What didya bring that book I don't want to be read to out of up for?" You'll have to try very hard to achieve such awkwardness, but try to avoid splitting the infinitive in the following sentence without making a change in the meaning:

> He will try to more than justify the cost of an assistant.
>
> ("Try to justify more than the cost" and "try more than to justify the cost" do not convey the meaning of the statement. *More than* must be located so that it clearly refers to *justify*.)

Where split infinitives and concluding prepositions are less awkward, use them; where they can be avoided without unnaturally warping the word order of the sentence, avoid them. There are far more important things to remember in achieving correct English than these minor points which have somehow attained a significance far beyond their worth.

The rest of this chapter attempts to do two things to help you write correct English:

1. *It selects 10 major principles which will aid you in avoiding the most frequent and most important errors in business writing.* This will give you a starting point, just as when you begin collecting classical records it is helpful to have a list of "the 10 classical records every music library must have." You may later decide you don't agree with the selection; they may not suit your tastes, or, in the case of the writing principles, your abilities. But, together with the topics discussed in Chapter 2, they will get you started.
2. *It reduces grammatical terminology to a minimum and, wherever possible, translates it into other terms.* You do have to know a certain amount of grammatical shoptalk, but not nearly so much as there is in a traditional handbook of grammar.

TEN MAJOR PRINCIPLES FOR CORRECTNESS

Subjects and Verbs

Since you express yourself in sentences and since you can't write a sentence without a *subject* and a *verb,* these words constitute a good place to begin. If you're an adult, you don't say "we is," "he are," or "you wasn't," although you may be guilty of "it don't," which means *it do not.* In English, certain subjects have acquired a tendency to "go steady" with certain verbs, and as a writer you will do well to avoid breaking up such long associations. The rule—and it's a hard and fast one—states that *verbs must agree with their subjects in number* ("singular," meaning *one;* "plural," meaning *more than one*) *and person* ("first person," *I, we;* "second person," *you;* "third person," *he, she, it, they*).

The rule is rather simple. The difficulties arise when you are not sure whether the subject of a verb is plural or singular or when you aren't sure even what the subject is. Principles 1 through 4 following are designed to help you in these situations.

Principle 1: Words intervening between the subject and verb do not affect the number of the verb.

Correct examples:

The manufacturing *processes,* which are under the direct control of the vice-president in charge of production at the head office, *are* extremely complex.

Particularly when you're dictating, you'll have a natural tendency to forget just what the subject of your sentence was and to think of intervening words—here, *control, production,* and *head office*—as affecting the number of the verb. They don't; and you should follow the same advice in handling this construction as the counsel given to speakers: *Keep your mind on the subject.*

Improvements in the annealing and cleaning process *were* a basic factor in this increased efficiency.

Here the subject, *improvements,* is plural; the intervening words are singular; and the businessman who originally wrote it succumbed to a tendency to let the last words affect his verb and used "was."

Principle 2: Words linked to the subject by expressions such as *together with, as well as, along with, including, and not,* **and** *in addition to,* **do not affect the number of the verb.**

Here, too, is an easy trap for dictators to fall into because of the tendency to lose sight of the subject.

Correct examples:

The office *manager,* as well as her two assistants and the three supervisors, *writes* concise reports.

This *example,* together with the ones cited in our last three reports, *shows* how important it is to correct this situation.

The *vice-president,* and not his reporting department head, *was* charged with this responsibility in the Procedures Manual.

The *statement* of policy, in addition to its general provisions, clauses, and applications, *is* wordy.

Principle 3: When the subject is any of the following words or is limited (modified) by them—*each, everybody, anybody, nobody, every, a person,* **and** *either***—the verb must be singular. When the subject is** *neither* **or** *none,* **the verb is almost always singular.**

Correct examples:

Each of these men *has* instituted several changes during the last month.

Everybody in this office *is* permitted to take a 15-minute coffee break at 10 o'clock.

Neither of us *wants* that to happen.

Current usage is recognizing plural verbs after *neither,* and you will find contructions using *neither* to link plural nouns. In the latter case, a plural verb is demanded:

Neither the men nor their wives *want* to stay.

A plural verb after *none* is well-accepted in constructions such as this:

None of our employees *are* so incompetent as the men in his department.

You might note, incidentally, that the indefinite *it* always takes a singular verb:

It is the workers who join unions.

Principle 4: When the subject is a collective noun, a word which by its meaning collects a lot of people or things—such as *committee, staff, company, crowd,* **and** *group*—**the meaning you wish to convey should determine whether the subject is singular or plural.**

When you are thinking of the parts, units, or individuals comprised in the collective, make your verb plural; when you are thinking of the collective as a whole, make your verb singular. You will use the singular more frequently, as:

The *group was* interested in investing in new plant facilities.

The *staff is* holding a monthly meeting to discuss sales forecasts.

Occasionally, you will want to emphasize the individuals, as in:

The executive *staff are* listed on page 42 of the annual report.

The *committee were* evenly divided in supporting the two policies.

Sometimes you will have difficulty in deciding between the singular and plural, and you may find yourself writing a sentence like this:

This *company is* good to work for; *they treat* you very fairly.

You are really thinking here of the people who make up the company; this is why you refer to the company as *they* and use a plural verb. There is something impersonal and perhaps a little ridiculous in "it treats you very fairly." Yet the expression "this company are good to work for" doesn't sound right, either. A hundred years ago it probably would have, because people thought of companies as groups of people. But today *company* means, to most people, a single business entity. Rather than be inconsistent and treat *company* as singular in one part of the sentence and plural in another, you should find some other phrasing altogether, such as: "This company is good to work for; the people here treat you very fairly."

Verbs

The verb is a remarkably versatile part of speech: It describes action or situation, tells time (by its *tense*), and provides a general background of assumptions (by its *mood*). It can describe reality (in the *indicative mood*), give commands (in the *imperative*), or express certain assumptions or statements that are not true (in the *subjunctive*). Besides all this, it adapts itself to performing the functions of other parts of speech. When *-ing* is added, the verb can function as a noun (a *gerund*) or remain a verb (a *participle*). This versatility adds importance to the need for knowing just which role the verb is playing.

In the next section, under "Danglers and Squinters," we will take a look at the participial form of verbs. Here we will discuss tenses, an aspect of verbs that often seems to leave business writers tied in knots. Be sure you know what the tenses of a verb look like. Then observe the rule:

Principle 5: Tenses of verbs in a sentence must indicate the correct sequence of actions, and the verb in a subordinate clause must take the tense demanded by the verb in the main clause.

If your sentence describes actions at different times, you must sort out the proper time sequence, decide what tense you want for the main clause, and then make the other clauses relate logically. For example:

When the machine *stopped,* the foreman *realized* that no one *had oiled* it.

The main clause is *the foreman realized,* and it is in the past tense. We imply that the stopping came simultaneously with the realizing. (If we wanted to make clear that the stopping came before the realizing, we would use *had stopped* rather than *stopped,* and *after* in place of *when.*) The second subordinate clause, *no one had oiled it,* describes an action that clearly preceded both the stopping and the realizing. Since we have chosen to put the realizing in the past, we must put the oiling in the past perfect.

Here are two incorrect examples:

When he *oiled* the machine, it *was ready* for service again. (The main clause is in the past tense, but the oiling had to take place before the machine was ready. The correct form is *had oiled.*)

When he *retires* this month, the foreman *will complete* ten years of work for the company and *will train* over a thousand men during those years.

We have a specific point of time in mind here—the foreman's retirement date. As of that time he will be able to look back on a training job completed: He *will have trained* over a thousand men. As it stands, the clause means he will train the men on his retirement day. We might quibble over *complete,* too, and argue that it should be *will have completed.* Does the foreman complete ten years of work the moment he retires or the moment before? The point doesn't seem important.

Frequently, words such as *after* and *before* and even *since, therefore,* and *because* clarify time relationships and eliminate reliance on tense to show sequence. Compare the following examples:

When he had come, I left.

After he came, I left.

Before he came, I left.

Because he came, I left.

The time sequence is quite clear in each sentence.

Danglers and Squinters

A dangling phrase is one that ought to refer to something in the sentence but doesn't. Most dangling phrases are participial phrases, hence the common term "dangling participle."

By adding -*ing* (as in writ*ing*) to a verb, or by placing *being* or *having* before it (as in *being seen* or *having done*), we form participles. When such forms function as nouns (as in "*writing* is hard work" or "*having* the work *done* was a source of satisfaction to him"), they are called *gerunds* or *gerundives*. Since participles get heavy use in letters and reports, you should watch them to see that they follow this rule:

> **Principle 6: When a participle is used in a phrase (such as** *"referring* **to your letter" or** *"reviewing* **these results"), there must be something appropriate for the phrase to modify, to cling to or depend on.**

Here is an example of a dangling participle:

Coming around the curve, the schoolhouse was seen.

Even if you change the word order, the schoolhouse is still seen to be coming around the curve. This is clearly nonsensical, but you are being equally illogical when you use any of the following constructions in your letters and reports:

Referring to your letter of March 25, the situation is being investigated.

Reviewing the results of the Greenpoint Plant, the same conclusions were reached.

It is only fair to point out that the meaning of these two sentences is probably clear, despite the dangling participles. For this reason, many business writers will defend the sentences as they stand and regard our criticism as characteristic of the "office pest." It may be that dangling participles will come to be accepted where there is no doubt as to what the reader means, but you are on safer ground when you avoid them. And unless you make a habit of avoiding them, you may find yourself using them to create unclear or even humorous statements, like that involving the moving schoolhouse, or like the following example from a London newspaper's description of a race won by a horse from the royal stables:

> Sired by the Royal Stallion, the Queen could not but feel satisfaction at the result.

Usually the dangling participle results from the use of the passive voice. One method of correcting the construction is to make the doer of the action in the participle serve as the subject of the sentence (ask yourself *who* is coming around the curve) and eliminate the passive voice:

> Coming around the curve, *we* saw the schoolhouse.

> Referring to your letter of March 25, *we* are investigating the situation.

> Reviewing the results of the Greenpoint Plant, *the committee* reached the same conclusions.

A second method of correcting the dangling construction is to change the phrase containing the participle to a clause (by giving it a subject and verb) and eliminate the participle.

> *When we came around the curve,* the schoolhouse was seen.

> *After the committee reviewed the results of the Greenpoint Plant,* the same conclusions were reached.

Sometimes a phrase which refers to something in the sentence, and is therefore not a dangler, is so located that the reader is prevented from seeing the reference clearly. For example:

> The testimonial dinner will be held in the grand ballroom of the hotel *consisting of the regular banquet fare.*

The italicized participial phrase modifies *dinner* and should be placed next to it.

The rule is simple:

Principle 7: Modifiers must be located so that it is clear what they modify.

We have already discussed the matter of logical location of the parts of a sentence in Chapter 2, under "Organization of a Sentence," so we won't deal with it any further here except to note the special problem of the "squinter." A squinter is a modifier located so that it might refer to more than one element in the sentence; the reader doesn't know which. For example:

> Even though it will take six years for the machines to pay for themselves, if conditions do not bring about a change in prices, the investment is decidedly attractive over the long run.

Does the *if* clause refer to *it will take six years* or to *the investment is attractive?*

Pronouns

If verbs and nouns play leading roles, pronouns may be called *stand-ins*. They take the place of nouns and serve the highly useful function of giving variety to such monotonous repetitions as this:

> Mr. Smith wrote a report in which Mr. Smith summed up the observations Mr. Smith made based on Mr. Smith's six months' stay at the Brookside Plant.

Troublesome as pronouns may be at times, this sentence should make you thankful that you can use them in your cast of characters. And their function as substitutes or stand-ins gives you the clue to why they are troublesome. Basically, your problem is to notify your reader without a shadow of doubt for *whom* or *what* your pronoun is substituting.

> When Mr. Smith reported the matter to the proper department head, he told him he would take action.

This is as bad a business sentence as you will ever see, because it fails to do what business communication must do: tell the reader clearly and unmistakably what the actual situation is. Who told whom? Who will take action? The reader doesn't know. Worse than ungrammatical, awkward, and nonstandard forms of English—bad as they are—is ambiguous English in business, and a large amount of this ambiguity derives from careless use of pronouns.

Reference of pronouns

A pronoun stands for a noun; the noun for which it stands is called its *antecedent.* Your prime responsibility when you use *he, she, it, they, who, which, this, that,* and other pronouns is to see that they refer unmistakably to their antecedents. There are certain exceptions. We can use *it,* for example, in an indefinite sense: "it rains," "it becomes more difficult," "it was felt," etc. But then we must be sure we don't create confusion by mixing an indefinite *it* with one intended to refer to something specific.

It (indefinite) is the responsibility of the management to see that *it* (supposed to refer to *management*) gets reports promptly; to do this, *it* (indefinite) is necessary to have *its* (management's?) report writers properly prepared.

The principle to keep in mind is this:

Principle 8: Pronouns must refer unmistakably to their antecedents, and relative pronouns—such as *who, which, that*—**must be placed as close as possible to their antecedents.**

Here are some incorrect examples:

We are sending you a check for the defective part which we hope will prove satisfactory. (Not the defective part, we hope, which has already proved unsatisfactory.)

During the second half of the discussion of Mr. Green's report, it was decided that it would be unnecessary to continue it. (Continue the report, the discussion?)

She had already informed the typist that she would be responsible for the general form of letters. (Who is responsible?)

Our economy of operation, achieved through an intensive work-simplification program, has eliminated the former high cost of production. This we can now pass on to our customers. (A new method of losing customers by handing them high costs.)

The supervisor told the young accountant that his statement was incorrect. (Whose statement?)

Selling has always been this young man's major interest, and that is why he is looking for employment as one in your company. (One what?)

We can correct these statements in this way:

We are sending you a check for the defective part, and we hope this adjustment is satisfactory to you.

During the second half of the discussion of Mr. Green's report, the committee decided that he need not continue the report (*or* decided that further discussion of the report was unnecessary).

The supervisor, who was responsible for the general form of letters, had already told the typist of this responsibility.

By getting rid of high production costs through an intensive work-simplification program, we have achieved greater economy of operation. The savings we can now hand on to our customers.

The young accountant's statement was incorrect, the supervisor told him.

Selling has always been this young man's major interest; that is why he wants to be a salesman in your company.

These examples show what you can do to clear up vague pronoun references. Occasionally you will have to repeat words, but repetition is better than ambiguity. Sometimes you will have to recast the whole sentence or break it into two sentences.

Case of pronouns

In their role as stand-ins for nouns, English pronouns have the troublesome trait of changing their garb when they perform different functions of the same role. If you think you have troubles as an English producer, though, you should be thankful that you aren't in charge of a language production in German or Latin, where four or six such changes are possible, or, to take an extreme, in Finnish, which has no less than fifteen cases! This functional change of garb is called *case*. When English nouns change case, they affect only one minor costume change. You can use *letter* as subject, as in "The letter was written," or as object, as in "He wrote the letter." The word remains the same. The only alteration is in the possessive, as in "The letter's style is objectionable." Your major attention to case, therefore, can be concentrated on certain pronouns. The terms used to describe the three cases illustrate their functions—*subjective, possessive, objective*. Here are the changes of case you ought to keep an eye on:

SUBJECTIVE—I	you	he	she	it	we	they	who	whoever
POSSESSIVE —my	your	his	her	its *	our	their	whose	whosever
OBJECTIVE —me	you	him	her	it	us	them	whom	whomever

* Not *it's*, which means "it is."

This is not an overwhelming list, and you are well-advised to keep it in mind and to place special emphasis on *who, whose,* and *whom,* which particularly plague business writers.

Principle 9: The form (case) of pronouns must suit their function, as follows:

a. *A pronoun as the object of a preposition must always take the objective case.* (Prepositions relate nouns or pronouns to some other word in the sentence. Among the most frequently used prepositions are *at, by, in, for, from, with, to, on, between, except, below, above,* and *under.*)

b. *A pronoun modifying a gerund uses the possessive case.* (A gerund is a verb used as a noun: "*Swimming* is good exercise.")

c. *A pronoun used to explain, to give in detail what is covered by another word* (this is called *apposition*), *takes the same case as the word which it explains.*

Here are examples. You might note that your intuition is especially likely to let you down here and lead you to incorrect constructions.

a. Between you and *me,* this must remain strictly confidential. (*Me* is object of the preposition *between.*)

This report did not agree with the previous one submitted by Mr. Jones and *her.* (*Her* is object of the preposition *by.*)

Copies were sent only to the executive staff and *him* as secretary. (*Him* is object of the preposition *to.*)

He has been a capable employee with *whom* I have worked closely. (*Whom* is object of the preposition *with.*)

No one from our company attended except Mr. Jones and *us.* (*Us* is object of the preposition *except.*)

b. We appreciated *your* writing us frankly. (*Writing* is a gerund; *your* is possessive.)

We did not learn about *his* being in the city until too late. (*Being* is a gerund; *his* is possessive.)

c. Three of us—Mr. Smith, Mr. Henry, and *me*—were asked to complete the report. (*Me* is in apposition with *us,* which is objective case.)

Only three employees could be located when the accident occurred—Mr. Smith, Mr. Henry, and *I.* (*I* is in apposition with *employees,* which is subjective case.)

There was some question as to whose responsibility it was—*his* or *mine.* (*Whose* is possessive; *his* and *mine* must be in the same case.)

You know that pronouns used as subjects of verbs are subjective case, and objects of verbs are objective case. Here are some situations affecting *who* and *whom* which cause difficulty:

He is one of the people *who,* I think, should be considered for the position. (The difficulty here arises from *I think,* which actually is a parenthetical kind of comment injected into the middle of the sentence. *Who* is the subject of *should be considered* and must be subjective case.)

He is the man *who,* you will remember, was interviewed last year. (This is like the previous sentence, with *you will remember* as the interjected parenthetical comment.)

On November 12, Mr. Smith, our representative, questioned the dealer as to *who* was responsible for this misunderstanding. (This type of involved sentence causes confusion because many writers think they must use *whom* as the object of the preposition *to.* Actually, your primary obligation is to provide a subject for the verb *was responsible.* This situation arises from the fact that an expression such as "the person" or "the individual" is understood, but not expressed, immediately before *who.* By saying this more simply, you can avoid all the confusion: "Mr. Smith questioned the dealer to find out who was responsible for the misunderstanding.")

We would appreciate your letting us know *whom* you addressed your reply to. (This usage shows some signs of breaking down, but in formal communication, such as letters and reports, you will do well to stick to the objective *whom* as object of the preposition *to.* The sentence could be improved and the case of *whom* made more obvious by moving the concluding preposition: "We would appreciate your letting us know to whom you addressed your reply.")

Our receptionist is instructed to jot down this information: *Who* called? *Whom* did he ask for? (*Whom* is objective after the preposition *for.* The best method of analyzing grammatical problems in interrogative sentences is either to turn them around: "He did ask for *whom,*" or to eliminate the concluding preposition: "For *whom* did he ask?" As in the previous example, this usage is breaking down. In speech we say "Who did he ask for?" but it is just as well to observe the rule in written communication.)

The pronoun and the conjunction *that*

There is a tendency among business writers, common enough that you should be warned of the error, to confuse the relative pronoun *that* with the conjunction *that.* This leads to such statements as:

We have just installed a new machine that the lubricating mechanism doesn't work.

The two uses of *that* are described in the rule:

Principle 10: Where a subordinate clause is introduced by *that,* **the main clause may not demand it to be a** *pronoun* **while at the same time the subordinate clause requires it to be a** *conjunction.*

In the example above, the main clause, "We have just installed a new machine," requires *that* to be a pronoun. We could write, correctly:

We have just installed a new machine that does not work properly.

But the subordinate clause demands *that* to be a conjunction. A correct sentence is:

We have found that the lubricating mechanism doesn't work.

The original example could be rewritten to preserve the main clause and the pronoun *that:*

We have just installed a new machine that suffers from a defective lubricating mechanism.

Or we could keep the original subordinate clause with the conjunction *that:*

We have just installed a new machine and discovered that the lubricating mechanism doesn't work.

Perhaps the best sentence avoids *that* altogether:

We have just installed a new machine, but the lubricating mechanism doesn't work.

A BRIEF WORD ABOUT SPELLING

Probably the worst offender against correctness is misspelled words. The ability to spell is assumed to be a universal acquisition of civilized people, like the ability to tie one's shoelaces or eat with a fork. Therefore, a reader can only suppose that the author of a poorly spelled report is either badly educated or contemptuous of the reader's opinion. No one wants to be thought uneducated, and very few young executives wish to insult their superiors. The solution obviously is to spell correctly.

This is easily accomplished with the aid of that faithful companion —the dictionary. Although there has been some recent controversy as to whether the dictionary makes the language or the language makes the dictionary, its reliability as a source of correct spelling is still unquestioned. We recommend that you own one and use it.

4

STYLED TO THE READER'S TASTE

We have discussed in the last three chapters the importance of thinking through the purpose of everything you write, and we have gone through the elements of clarity and correctness. Once you know what you are doing, once your writing is clear and correct, isn't this adequate? For many purposes, it may be. But if your aim is to persuade your reader to your point of view, to make him act, to impress him with your knowledge or your reasoning powers or the effort you have put into your work, you must first capture his attention. The quality in writing which compels attention we call *style*.

Written communication must be a two-way street. It does not do you much good to write if no one is going to read. Much of the time you can be pretty sure that what you have written will be read or, at least, that someone will begin to read it. Most of your writing will concern things your reader wants to know about. This is not true in advertising, of course, where your job is rather similar to the job of the literary writer. There you must often struggle to convince your reader that what you have written is worth reading. But for the most part you have the advantage that your subject matter will interest your reader enough to get him started.

Although business writers can generally assume this ready-made interest, they must also remember this: When we ask a reader to pay too dearly for what he is getting, we not only lose his interest but also squander his principal, the time he invests. Exorbitant demands by writers result in skimming, skipping, and frustration and reflect anything but credit on the writer.

An effective writer learns to capitalize on the reader's initial interest and to hold it throughout his communication. To do this, the writer must understand his reader. The degree of understanding will, of course, vary in different situations. If you are writing reports and memorandums for the same people frequently, you will come to know a good deal about your readers and you will have the added advantage of feedback—their comments on how well you are doing.

Such personal contact occurs less frequently when you write business letters. Often you will know very little about your reader, and you may never receive a reaction to your letter. But lack of familiarity with your reader is no excuse for ignoring him when you write. In fact, it is additional reason for thinking through carefully what a reader probably is looking for in your writing and what the probable effect of what you have written will be on most readers.

Understanding your reader does not require any elaborate feats of psychology. It is a good idea to steer clear of such theories as the one that American people have an average mental age of twelve years. Except in special situations, such as when you are trying to decide whether to use technical language, it is safest to assume that your reader thinks somewhat as you do, that his understanding is about the same, that he appreciates clarity and conciseness as much as you do, and that he objects to condescension as much as you would.

You may miss your mark occasionally. When you do, remember that the reaction of readers can at times be totally unexpected. The collection agent for a furniture store learned this when he sent the following letter to a delinquent debtor:

Dear Mr. Smith:

What would your neighbors think if we have to send our truck out to your house to repossess that furniture on which you have not met your last three payments?

Sincerely yours,
The Acme Furniture Co.

A week later he received this answer:

Dear Sir:

I have discussed the matter you wrote me about with all of my neighbors and every one of them thinks it would be a mean, low-down trick.

Yours truly,
John Smith

The following principles can guide you to a style appropriate to most business communication. They have a common goal: to make it as easy as possible for the reader to understand and become interested in your writing.

1. Write on the level of your reader's understanding.
2. Be concise.
3. Watch your pace.
4. Keep your sentences short.
5. Put your qualifying ideas in separate sentences.
6. Use paragraphs to break your text into readable units.

7. Avoid too much use of the passive voice.
8. Use verbs.
9. Be direct.
10. Keep your tone appropriate.
11. Be specific.

Write on the Level of Your Reader's Understanding

If there is one fundamental characteristic of life in the twentieth century which affects our writing, it is the overwhelming trend toward specialization. An inevitable result of this specialization is fragmentation of knowledge; and since language is the tool of thought, the only means of transmitting knowledge, it, too, has fragmented into technical, specialized units. Thus every profession, every skill, has developed a little language all its own. The doctor speaks of "spasmodic torticollis" when he means a twisted neck, and none but doctors can understand him. The metallurgist speaks of "dilatimetric research," which really means the study of what happens when metal stretches, but his words might just as well be Greek to those who are not metallurgists. These special languages, used properly, are valuable. But it should be obvious that what is appropriate when one doctor talks to another is not always appropriate when a doctor talks to his patient.

Here are excerpts from two reports on the same accident written for a reader with no technical knowledge. The first is by a recent college graduate, the second by an experienced writer who knew what his reader wanted and how much he would understand:

a. An 11-KV distribution cable faulted to ground in the subway cable duct in close proximity to the substation. A high thermal condition developed in the oil circuit-breaker when this piece of equipment attempted to interrupt the excessive current in the faulted circuit. As a result, the gasified oil created sufficient pressure inside the circuit-breaker tank to rupture the tank and ignite the oil that was projected over everything within a radius of approximately 20 feet. The fault was ultimately cleared by multiple tripping that deenergized the affected 11-KV section of the station.

The necessity to extinguish the conflagration prevented immediate transfer and restoration of service to the affected area. The delay in restoration was approximately ten minutes.

b. The cable shorted to ground near the substation, blew up the oil switch and set fire to the station. It took ten minutes to put out the fire and restore service.

What has all this to do with learning to write in business? A great deal, really, for the chances are excellent that you already know some shoptalk or that you will quickly acquire some on the job. This second language can create more confusion or more clear-cut communication than any other tool you use in writing. The two possible extremes result directly from how much your reader understands. As a writer, you must learn to avoid two major pitfalls—overestimating your reader's understanding and confusing him with highly specialized technical language, or underestimating his understanding and annoying him with patronizingly childish terms.

Unwillingness to assess the reader's understanding, and consequent failure to write to him in his language, is surprisingly frequent. A large bank writes to customers "explaining" that "the installment manager will put a bring-up on your file for the 15th." A big department store sends collection letters to customers saying, "Your account is still open on our records and we, therefore, anticipate a remittance." A manufacturer writes, "Have you notified C and A group?" But how many average readers know that "bring-up on your file" is technical jargon for "We will send you a reminder," that "open on our records" means you haven't paid your bill, and that "C and A group" is shoptalk for the claims and adjustment department?

The classic story about such communication failures—and even if you have heard it, it will bear repeating—concerns a plumber who had found hydrochloric acid excellent for cleaning drains. He wrote a Washington bureau to find out if it was harmless. Replied Washington.

> The efficacy of hydrochloric acid is indisputable, but the chlorine residue is incompatible with metallic permanence.

The plumber wrote back, thanked the bureau, and said he was very glad they agreed that hydrochloric acid was effective. Back came the second reply:

We cannot assume responsibility for the production of toxic and noxious residues from hydrochloric acid, and we suggest, therefore, that some alternative procedure be used.

The plumber answered that he was getting fine results thus far and that he thought the bureau might like to suggest the use of hydrochloric acid to other people. Finally, someone in Washington exploded into simple language understandable to the reader:

Don't use hydrochloric acid; it eats hell out of the pipes.

There are times when you simply cannot avoid using highly technical language. For example, legal documents are usually written in terms almost incomprehensible to the nonlawyer. This is for a good reason. The lawyer who writes the document has something to say, and he wants to say it precisely, leaving no ambiguities and no room for interpretation. He has a language which is admirably suited to this purpose. Here, for example, is a single sentence from the Internal Revenue Code:

SECTION 904 (f) (4) (B)

Where, under the provisions of subsection (d), taxes (i) paid or accrued to any foreign country or possession of the United States in any taxable year beginning on or before the date of the enactment of the Revenue Act of 1962 are deemed (ii) paid or accrued in one or more taxable years beginning after the date of the enactment of the Revenue Act of 1962, the amount of such taxes deemed paid or accrued in any year described in clause (ii) shall, with respect to interest income described in paragraph (2), be an amount which bears the same ratio to the amount of such taxes deemed paid or accrued as the amount of the taxes paid or accrued to such foreign country or possession for such year with respect to interest income described in paragraph (2) bears to the total amount of the taxes paid or accrued to such foreign country or possession for such year; and the amount of such taxes deemed paid or accrued in any year described in clause (ii) with respect to income other than interest income described in paragraph (2) shall be an amount which bears the same ratio to the amount of such taxes deemed paid or accrued for such year as the amount of taxes paid or accrued to such foreign country or possession for such year with respect to income other than interest income described in paragraph (2) bears to the total amount of the taxes paid or accrued to such foreign country or possession for such year.

If you can understand this sentence after four or five readings, you are doing extremely well. It is the kind of writing that can drive even skilled lawyers to drink. Yet if you study it long enough, you will discover that it says very efficiently and very clearly just what its draftsman had in mind. It would be possible to express the ideas in this excerpt in language more easily understood by ordinary readers. But it would not be possible to combine easy readability with the precision of the original without using a great many more words. What a lawyer may do, and what you may have to do where absolute precision of language is demanded, is to provide two statements: a technical, precise one and an easily read interpretation. It is often difficult to decide how much precision to sacrifice to achieve a readable yet reasonably brief statement.

Sometimes, of course, the writer who uses very technical language has no desire to explain it to the ordinary reader. There are plenty of stories about lawyers who put contracts and wills in easy-to-understand language. Their clients, who expected impressively incomprehensible documents, were disappointed and turned to others for counsel. As a business writer, however, you are not likely to lose customers because you write clearly and simply. The use of technical language merely for the sake of its impressive sound is something most readers can do without.

Let just one example suffice to illustrate attempts to impress. A consultant on communication was being escorted through the offices of a company by its vice-president when they came to the room which housed the central files of the company. Turning to a file clerk, the consultant asked, "How long do you keep things in these files?" "Normally we don't keep forms no more than three years. Then you can either tear them up yourself or give them to the janitor." The visitor turned to the vice-president. "When we get back to your office, let's see how this situation is described in the Procedures Manual." And here is what the manual said:

At the end of the established retention period, which is normally three years, mutilate the forms or carbons to be destroyed by tearing them into small bits or pieces or by shredding them, and dispose of the resulting waste in accordance with the procedures established for the Maintenance Department.

Whoever wrote that statement was attempting to make a relatively simple task sound impressive and complex. The words of the file clerk, despite her bad grammar, are a far more effective explanation because she tried to express an idea rather than to impress a listener.

We can sum up the discussion so far by saying that since your objective is to have your writing understood, you must estimate the level of your reader's understanding and write on that level. Here are some simple points to keep in mind.

1. If you know your reader is a specialist and speaks your technical language, you can communicate in your common shoptalk to your heart's content. In fact, if you do not, he may feel you are talking down to him and failing to appreciate his understanding.
2. If you are not sure of your reader's familiarity with your special language, stick to simple, everyday English. If you can't avoid technical terms, define or explain them carefully.
3. Refrain from using technical language merely to impress your reader.

Be Concise

Good writing, says an old adage, is the art of speaking volumes without writing them. In business writing, you should write not only so your reader will understand, but also so he will understand as quickly and easily as possible. Don't tax his attention with a sentence such as this:

During the past two weeks, we have been wondering if you have as yet found yourself in a position to give us an indication of whether you have been able to come to a decision on our offer.

This statement uses too many words to say: "Have you decided on our offer?"

Being concise is not the same as being brief. A brief report, memorandum, or letter usually contains only the highlights or bare essentials of what the writer has to say. A concise piece of writing may contain any amount of detail and be very long. But it is efficient: It conveys all the writer wishes to say in the shortest, most direct way. It enables the reader to comprehend as quickly and easily as possible what is said.

Consider this example. An applicant for a job writes:

Two considerations influence my choice of a job: pay and working hours.

What does this tell the employer? Almost everyone is influenced to some extent in his choice of a job by the amount he will be paid. Is this applicant especially concerned about money? And is he influenced by the number of hours he will work or by the particular time —night or day shift, for example?

Here is a more complete, but no less concise, revision:

Two considerations influence my choice of a job: the hourly rate and the number of hours I work.

Much of the original ambiguity and vagueness is gone. We may still wonder whether the applicant is afraid he will be asked to work too many hours or whether he is anxious to make more money by working extra hours. Here is an even more complete, yet still concise, version:

Two considerations influence my choice of a job: my unwillingness to accept less than $2 an hour and my desire to work at least four hours overtime each week.

The original example is briefer than the second and third, but it is no more concise and much less complete. It lacks the efficiency we have built into the second and third versions, where we have said much more, achieved precision, and eliminated ambiguity.

A lack of conciseness often results when a writer's fingers become itchy before he has thought through what he wants to say. Here is a sentence written while the writer was getting ready to think:

The advantages of centralized production are decidedly in favor of centralized manufacturing.

"Blessed is the man," says George Eliot, "who, having nothing to say, abstains from giving in words evidence of the fact."

Irrelevancy is a major enemy of conciseness. A writer almost always tends to go on at great length about the things that interest him. And most of us are vain enough to wish to display our knowledge of the subject we are discussing. The result may be that much of what is written appears quite irrelevant to the reader, whose needs do not necessarily fit the writer's interests and who has no desire to wade through a display of proficiency.

Here is a portion of an auditor's report to a comptroller on incorrect procedures he discovered in a company's payroll department:

I have discovered what is, in effect, a mishandling of funds. Employees are permitted to authorize payroll deductions for savings bonds, in accordance with a decision reached during the Korean conflict, when the Board of Directors decided to encourage bond purchases as a patriotic gesture. At the end of that crisis no change was made in the policy, probably because many employees were purchasing bonds and the company likes to see them building security for emergencies and their old age. The deductions are posted to savings bond accounts, and when an employee's account is large enough, a bond is purchased for him. Some employees have discovered that the payroll is actually made up quite early in the month and that the savings bond deductions are posted at this time to the employees' savings bond accounts. It has always been company policy to permit an employee to withdraw from his account any savings bond deductions that have not yet actually been used to buy bonds. This policy was established at the insistence of the Treasurer, who has been with the company for twenty-three years and has worked in every one of our plants. He felt the money in the accounts was still the employees' and that they should be able to do as they like with it. The employees referred to above, who have learned of the posting procedure, withdraw amounts from their savings bond accounts as soon as the postings are made, long before payday. Thus they obtain, in effect, an advance salary payment.

It seems unlikely that the comptroller needed to know the history of the payroll deduction plan or the details of the treasurer's past life. What he did need to know was (1) that employees were allowed to authorize payroll deductions for bond purchases, (2) that the deductions were posted to individual accounts well before payday, (3) that withdrawals were permitted as soon as postings had been made, and (4) that some employees were making these withdrawals and in effect receiving advance payments of salary. The preceding 50 words convey all that is relevant to the comptroller's needs, out of the 255-word statement. You may feel that the 50-word summary is a little too abbreviated, but you can expand it considerably without coming close to the length of the original. Length, as such, however, is not here the important criterion of conciseness. The trouble with the example is not merely its length but also the way in which the reader is distracted—taken away from what he wants to know more about and forced to read information he has no use for.

Jargon is another great enemy of conciseness. We referred to jargon in the preceding chapter, in connection with the need to select the word that conveys precisely what you mean. Jargon is not only vague; it clutters otherwise concise writing and prevents the reader from quickly grasping what you have to say.

Fortunately, a great deal of progress has been made recently in reducing the number of jargoneers. The very fact that business has become conscious of jargon is a hopeful sign. But much remains to be done. An amazing collection of strange, meaningless, trite, and pompous expressions has persisted in business writing, chiefly because untrained writers sit down to write letters with only the incoming correspondence and the hackneyed reports in the files to guide them. Executives who pride themselves on their efficiency and on the forcefulness of their speaking lapse in writing into the stilted style known as business jargon. The same man who would phone a business friend and say, in a natural way, "I'm sending a check for $110.15 along to you today. Thanks for being so patient about this," is all too likely to write a letter dealing with the same situation in a formal, pompous tone:

Dear Sir:
With reference to your letter of November 21, addressed to our Treasurer, in connection with our account, we are remitting

herewith our check as per your statement in the amount of $110.15. Please be advised that according to our records our account with you is paid to date. We also wish to express our appreciation for your consideration in this matter.

Yours truly,

To those unacquainted with business, this may sound like an absurd exaggeration; actually, it is all too typical.

TRITE AND OUTWORN EXPRESSIONS TO AVOID

The following is a list of the more common expressions included in business jargon. Beginning writers should consider them as warnings of bad habits they may fall into; experienced writers may use them as a yardstick against which they can measure the effectiveness of their diction.

Acknowledge receipt of—as in "We wish to acknowledge receipt of the data." Forget it; say "Thank you for your data."

Advise—as in "In answer to your letter of August 7, we wish to advise that shipment has been made." "Advise" is a perfectly good word, but it means "to give advice"; in general, it should be replaced by "inform" when information is being conveyed.

Allow me to—as in "Allow me to express our appreciation for." A pompous method of saying "Thank you for."

Along these lines—as in "We are carrying on research along these lines." A meaningless phrase. Make it specific.

As a matter of fact—Five unnecessary words with the implication that other statements in the letter or report are not matters of fact.

As per—as in "As per our records," "As per your report," etc. Another barbarous mixture; say "According to."

Attached please find—No hunting is necessary if your check or order is attached. Say "We are attaching" or "We enclose our check" and let it go at that.

At an early date, at the earliest possible moment—Say "soon" and save yourself some words.

At hand—as in "I have your letter of May 9 at hand." Omit it entirely since "at hand" adds nothing. "Thank you for your letter of May 9" or better "Your letter of May 9. . . ."

At the present writing, at this time—Overworked and roundabout jargon for "now."

At your earliest convenience—Say "soon" and save yourself some words.

Awaiting your favor—This might make a song title, but you probably mean "We hope to hear from you soon" or "Please let us hear from you."

Beg—as in "Beg to inform," "Beg to acknowledge," "Beg to state," "Beg to remain," etc. Omit "beg" entirely. Go ahead and inform, acknowledge, state, or remain; it is absurd for perfectly solvent firms to go around begging in their business letters.

Contents duly noted—as in "Your favor received and contents duly noted." Say "Thank you for your letter or report" and let it go at that.

Dictated but not read—Of all the insulting notations on letters, this is the worst. Readers who receive them should immediately write back "Received but not read."

Enclosed please find—as in "Enclosed please find our check for $25." He won't have to hunt for your check if it *is* enclosed; simply say "We enclose" or "We are enclosing."

Even date, current date, recent date—as in "Your memo of even date." Give the specific date. "Your memo of January 12."

Favor—as in "Thank you for your favor of October 22" or "In response to your favor of July 10." Never call a letter a "favor"; call it what it is—a letter.

For your information—Tactless. Everything in the report or letter is for his information. Omit it.

Hand you—as in "We herewith hand you our check for $37.10." A meaningless and outworn expression—and what long arms you have, Grandma! Say "We enclose our check for $37.10."

I have your letter, I have received your report—A thoughtless warm-up for starting letters or memos. Since you are answering, he knows you have the letter. Say "Thank you for your report" or "We appreciate your letter of February 15."

In receipt of—as in "We are in receipt of your check." Say "We have received your check" or "Thank you for your check."

In (or to or for) the amount of—as in "We enclose our check in the amount of $33.16." Simply say "for" as in "We enclose our check for $33.16."

In the near future—Be specific, or save words with "soon."

Permit me to say—Go on and say it; no permission is needed.

Thanking you in advance—as in "Thanking you in advance for any information you may send." Poor psychology because it antagonizes the reader by too obviously assuming that he is going to do what you want him to. Say "We shall be grateful for any information you may care to send."

Thank you kindly—An absurd statement. Why are you being kind in thanking him? Just say "Thank you."

The writer—as in "The writer believes" or "It is the opinion of the writer." An obvious and pompous attempt to give the impression of modesty by avoiding the use of "I" or "we." Don't be afraid to use "I believe" or "We think."

This letter is for the purpose of requesting—Why all this preliminary? Go ahead and ask. When you write effective letters, their purpose is clear.

This will acknowledge receipt of your letter—Another wasted warm-up.

Under separate cover—as in "We are sending under separate cover." This should be used very sparingly; whenever possible be specific. "We are sending by parcel post (or express or air mail)."

The undersigned—See comments on "the writer." Say "I."

Up to this writing—Say "Up to now."

We regret to inform you that we are in error—Wordy and hackneyed. Say "We are sorry for our mistake."

You claim, you state, you say—Avoid these wherever possible because they antagonize the reader by implying that his statement is not true. Recast the sentence to eliminate them.

Yours—as in "Yours of recent date." Say "Your letter" or "Your order."

These are the specters that haunt business communication. But the jargoneer has other devices to assure pompousness. Above all else, he enjoys using several words where one or two are necessary, and he likes to say the same thing twice by using what are known as *doublets*. Just as he prefers "in the amount of" to "for," he selects the following wordy expressions in the left-hand column rather than those in the right, which effective writers use.

Answer in the affirmative	*say yes*
At a later date	*later*
At the present time	*now*
Despite the fact that	*though, although*
Due to the fact that	*since, because*
For the purpose of	*to, for*
For the reason that	*since, because*
In accordance with your request	*as you requested*
In addition	*also*
Inasmuch as	*since*
In order that	*so*
In order to	*to*
In the event that	*if*

In the nature of	*like*
In the neighborhood of	*about*
In the normal course of our procedure	*normally*
In the very near future	*soon*
In this connection	omit
In this day and age	*today*
In view of the fact that	*since, because*
Of the order of magnitude of	*about*
On the grounds that	*because*
On the occasion of	*when, on*
Prior to	*before*
Pursuant to our agreement	*as we agreed*
Subsequent to	*after*
The reason is due to	*because*
Under date of	*on*
We are not in a position to	*we cannot*
Will you be kind enough to	*please*
With a view to	*to*
Without further delay	*now, immediately*
With reference to	*about*
With regard to	*about*
With respect to	*about*
With the result that	*so that*

Equally dear to the hearts of jargoneers are redundant phrases. Here are a few examples.

Absolutely complete	*complete*
Agreeable and satisfactory	just one
Anxious and eager	one or the other
Basic fundamentals	*fundamentals,* being basic, will suffice
Consensus of opinion	*consensus* can't be anything but opinion; say just *consensus*
Courteous and polite	one or the other, not both
Each and every one of us	*each of us, every one of us, all of us*
Exactly identical	*identical*
First and foremost	either one, not both

Full and complete	just one
Hope and trust	*hope*
If and when	either one
Insist and demand	choose one
My personal opinion	*my opinion;* it can't be anything but personal
Right and proper	don't say the same thing twice
Sincere and earnest	select one
Thought and consideration	only one
True facts	since facts are true, omit the adjective
Unique—as "the most unique," "very unique," etc.	*unique* cannot be qualified; it means one of a kind, without equal

Watch Your Pace

Inside the doors of buses in a certain city appears this cryptic statement: "Pay enter East Pay leave West." Habitual riders are accustomed to seeing strangers to the city snarled at by bus drivers when they try to find out when to pay their fare or when, still worse, they drop it into the box at the wrong time. There is both a complete failure of communication and a ducking of responsibility by irritated drivers, who wearily point to the signs as if the instructions were simple English. What the signs really mean is: When you are on a bus going east, pay when you enter the bus; when you are going west, pay when you leave. Since strangers usually can't figure out what the signs mean and don't even know whether the buses are going east or west, utter confusion results. Contrast the statement with the sign one bus driver lettered on his fare box: "Don't fumble while others grumble. Please pay exact fare 18¢ when you get on," and you have the difference between inadequate and effective communication.

The first example is an illustration of poor pacing—trying to say too much in too few words. Whenever you see someone puzzling over how to operate a vending machine, how to follow a receptionist's instructions for getting from one office to another, or how to run an automatic elevator, poor pacing may be responsible. The instructions go too fast for the reader; they attempt to say too much in too few words, or they wrongly assume that everyone understands the short cuts in language. Occasionally, terseness and compression of several ideas in one sentence are effective changes of pace, but this sort of writing requires great skill. Here is an example from *Time:*

> In Chilliwack, B.C., Mrs. Edna Fenton walked into police headquarters and asked the desk constable how she might get herself jailed to escape her angry husband, was advised to hit a cop, did, was.

Unless you are a very able writer, you will do well to avoid trying to pack too much information into your sentences.

The opposite fault in pacing occurs when a few meager facts or ideas are strung out on a long clothesline of words. In business writing slow pacing occurs more frequently than fast pacing. Here's an example from a business report which moves at a snail's pace:

> Since the beginning of large-scale research programs on automatic controls, there has been a need for simple but rapid tests to evaluate these controls. These methods of evaluation must be easy to use and fast. They should also give a definite answer. What is needed is a method which says "yes" or "no" to a specific problem of using automatic controls. The current emphasis on these controls has posed a difficult problem in the field of their evaluation. We, therefore, need evidence which will give us a method of deciding when to use them.

Such slow-paced writing creates a knotty problem for the reader. The first time he reads it, he gets a vague impression that the writer is actually saying something significant. Then, if he is patient and goes back to examine what has been said, he finds that 6 sentences and 95 words have been expended to express one simple idea:

> Because of the widespread use of automatic controls, we need to develop a simple, fast, and definite method of evaluating their use.

Here is another example, this one from a text on financial management:

Financial management is the responsibility for obtaining and effectively utilizing the funds necessary for the efficient operation of an enterprise. The finance function centers about the *management* of funds—raising and using them effectively. But the dimensions of financial management are much broader than simply obtaining funds. Planning is one of the most important activities of the financial manager.

This writer started out with what he thought was a fairly good definition of financial management, and he put it in the first sentence. But evidently he was not satisfied that he had made himself clear, so he said the same thing again, in different words, in his second sentence. He seems then to have decided that his definition was not really complete. In his third sentence, he prepared to expand on it, but in doing so he partly recapitulated his original definition, so that the reader doesn't know whether more repetition or a new thought is on the way. Finally, in his fourth sentence, he completed his definition. What the whole paragraph seems to mean is:

The financial manager has the responsibility for obtaining and effectively utilizing the funds necessary for the efficient operation of an enterprise. Planning is one of his most important activities.

Keep Your Sentences Short

How short is "short"? No simple answer will suffice; Dr. Rudolph Flesch, who wrote *The Art of Plain Talk,* believes that an *average* sentence length of 17 words makes for high readability. Writers in business should aim at variety in both the length and pattern of their sentences. They should occasionally check the average length of sentences in their letters and reports to see that it falls somewhere between 15 and 20 words. If not, they should employ a very useful device—the period—more frequently; most long sentences lend themselves logically to this chopping-up process.

I should greatly appreciate your letting me know what your decision is so that I can send the report to Mr. Jones in our

Memphis office with a request for more information which we will need to make our plans for the coming year and to encourage him to make any suggestions he may want to incorporate. (*One sentence, 57 words*)

I should greatly appreciate your letting me know your decision. I can then send the report to Mr. Jones in our Memphis office requesting more information. We will need his suggestions for next year's plans. (*Three sentences, 35 words*)

Perhaps the best analysis of why sentences should be kept short and clear is this statement by Herbert Spencer in his *Philosophy of Style:*

A reader or listener has at each moment but a limited amount of mental power available. To recognize and interpret the symbols presented to him requires part of this power; to arrange and combine the images suggested requires a further part; and only that part which remains can be used for realizing the thought conveyed. Hence, the more time and attention it takes to achieve and understand each sentence, the less time and attention can be given to the contained idea; and the less vividly will that idea be conceived. . . .

This analysis of what happens when the reader reads is a good argument for carrying the reader along step by step. Don't force him to go along until he is breathless from the sheer length of your sentences. By doing so, you merely divert the small amount of attention he has left for comprehending.

Put Your Qualifying Ideas in Separate Sentences

Paradoxically, one of the worst attributes of business writing stems from an admirable human quality—the desire to write the exact, absolute, and final truth in a sentence. But since a sentence follows a pattern of one thought at a time, it is impossible to express all kinds of qualifications and conditions without producing a long, complex, and highly involved sentence. "And you become obscure," said Aristotle, "if, in seeking to introduce a number of details in the middle of a sentence, you do not complete the sense before you mention them." This zeal for accuracy throws ideas or information at the reader at too fast a pace. Notice this example:

> The result of this study is a recommendation that our hiring policies should be changed during the coming year but it should be remembered that this recommendation may not be sound if there is an appreciable change in the labor market during that period or if changing circumstances affect our own company's level of operations so that we need to increase or decrease the total number of employees.

You can always spot this kind of long-windedness by such words as *under certain circumstances, under different conditions,* and similar phrases. They are almost inevitable in these sentences because that is just what the writer attempts to do—to take care of all the possible contingencies, conditions, or variable elements in one sentence. As we have suggested, the cause may be his own intellectual honesty or it may be the opposite—a desire to hedge, to avoid committing himself unequivocally. Whatever the cause, don't clutter your sentences with too many qualifying ideas. Break such sentences as the one cited above like this:

> The result of our study is a recommendation to change our hiring policies during the coming year. This recommendation may not be sound if the labor market changes in the next year or if unforeseen business conditions affect our company's level of operations. If that happens, we will have to change the number of employees.

The classic definition of the sentence is *a group of words to convey a single thought.* Too many writers in business err on the side of putting qualifying phrases and clauses into their sentences and hence lengthen them to a point which passeth understanding. Aim at conciseness, at clean-cut sentences, and put the qualifiers in separate sentences. Schopenhauer expressed the reaction of most readers when he commented: "In these long sentences rich in involved parentheses, like a box of boxes within one another, and padded out like roast geese stuffed with apples, it is really the memory that is chiefly taxed."

Fundamentally, the sentence is the basic test of how clearly you think. It can be a hazy, vague, flabby collection of words or a functional, well-designed garb for a thought. The result will depend on how much thinking you have done before you write. Great writers have always recognized this inexorable link between clear thinking and effective writing. Perhaps the best illustration of this concerns Richard Brinsley Sheridan, the famous dramatist who wrote *The School for Scandal* and *The Rivals*. A friend asked him how his new play was coming along. "It's finished," said Sheridan. "When can I read the script?" asked his friend. "Oh, I haven't written a word yet," Sheridan replied. And that is where good sentences are "written" first—in your mind.

Use Paragraphs to Break Your Text into Readable Units

Readers in the twentieth century have become accustomed to seeing material in smaller units than those used a century ago. Advertisers, journalists, and other writers have, therefore, learned to break text into shorter and more readable units. You can test this practice on the basis of your own habits when you read a novel. If you are typical, the chances are that you read most of the conversation and skim over most of the description. You do this not because the conversation is necessarily more interesting than the description but because it generally comes in shorter units of text.

When you write reports, letters, or memorandums, you should remember that long paragraphs, heavy chunks of typing or print, have an eye-repelling quality for today's reader. They should be divided into more easily comprehended bits by a technique which advertising men call *letting daylight into the copy*.

No one can say authoritatively how long a paragraph should be; that will depend entirely on how thoroughly or in how much detail you are trying to develop an idea or a topic. It will also depend on the reader, whose preferences in business writing we have already discussed. Certainly you will be exacting too high a payment of attention from most business readers if you write paragraphs which cover a whole page. At the opposite extreme, you don't want paragraphs averaging only a sentence or two because you then won't be developing your ideas as you should.

To be completely practical, most long paragraphs in business communication can be broken up without any loss of their logic; in fact, most of these paragraphs are written because the writer has lost sight of his reader and of the way he reads. In reports and memorandums, therefore, you can use an arbitrary rule of thumb by trying to break the text into at least three or four paragraphs on a page.

Avoid Too Much Use of the Passive Voice

Excessive use of the passive voice results in more wordiness in business writing than almost any other form of expression. It results, too, in monotony, vagueness, and complete lack of vigor. The passive has its uses. You may find that older readers and technically trained men, such as engineers and accountants, prefer an impersonal, passive style because they were schooled in that tradition. The tradition, however, is breaking down. A better reason for using the passive voice is to achieve an unemphatic, impersonal style in the specific cases where this suits your purpose. Rather than point a finger of accusation, for example, you may prefer a little vagueness. Compare these two examples:

> The sales manager has permitted unauthorized expenditures on advertising.

> Unauthorized expenditures have been made on advertising.

To a reader who understands the company's organization, the two sentences may mean the same thing. The first is vigorous, very explicit, and would be recommended by most text writers. The second, however, may suit your purposes better.

Note that it is all too easy to take refuge in the passive to avoid admitting your own responsibilities:

> An overestimate of sales last year has produced an inventory level higher than normal.

> I made a bad estimate of sales last year and now our inventory is too high.

You might prefer to write the first sentence, but a reader who understands your responsibilities will quickly see your attempt to cover up.

On the whole there is far too much use of the passive in business writing. Writers get into the habit of using the passive voice, perhaps because of a constant unwillingness to be specific and commit themselves emphatically, perhaps because they have read so much business and technical material written in the passive. Here is an unfortunately typical construction from a business report:

> When our employees are subjected to long work hours which are necessitated by storms, it is expected that a higher rate of accidents will prevail.

What this writer means is:

> When storms force our employees to work long hours, we can expect a higher accident rate.

Unless you have a specific need for the passive voice, stick to the active except for occasional variation. But let the passive be the variation, not the theme. Here are examples in which the active voice improves a statement:

Passive: It is noted that the sales volume has been increasing.

Active: We note that the sales volume has increased.

Passive: It is believed that this policy will be beneficial to our personnel.

Active: We believe this policy will benefit our personnel.

Passive: Consideration is being given to this matter by our Sales Department.

Active: Our Sales Department will consider this matter.

Passive: It is occasionally found that one of our customers has been unintentionally missed by our representative.

Active: Occasionally, our representative unintentionally misses one of our customers.

Use Verbs

We have seen how the active voice can put life and vigor into your writing and cut away excess verbiage. Much the same can be accomplished by making verbs carry the load of what you have to say. The vividness of Sir Winston Churchill's writing is due in large part to his reliance on verbs and to his choice of strong, expressive verbs. Participles, infinitives, and adjectives carry much less force than active verbs. Even nouns are frequently less effective than well-chosen verbs. Notice this statement of conclusions from a report:

> It was found that by selection of the proper test conditions it was possible to duplicate the actual use of the machine by the housewife. Under these conditions, there was a definite tendency for the fan mechanism to deteriorate or to break down completely after usage which was equivalent to $3\frac{1}{2}$ years of service in the home. It is believed, therefore, that it is desirable to replace the fan mechanism by substituting the larger motor which is capable of 6 years of service under the same conditions.

These 87 words virtually stand still, but by inserting some strong verbs, and especially by replacing infinitives, we can give the paragraph both conciseness and forward movement.

> By selecting proper test conditions, we duplicated the housewife's actual use of the machine. These tests showed that the fan mechanism deteriorated or broke down after the equivalent of $3\frac{1}{2}$ years of service in the home. We believe the larger motor should be used because our tests show it can give 6 years of service under the same conditions.

Notice how these sentences from letters and memorandums can be improved by putting verbs to work:

> *Instead of:* Application of these principles is the best way for us to obtain the cooperation of our retailers.
>
> *Say:* By applying these principles, we can get our retailers to cooperate.

Instead of: This sales message is something of vital concern to all our personnel.

  Say: This sales message vitally concerns all our personnel.

Instead of: This contract has a requirement that it be signed by you.

  Say: This contract requires your signature.

Instead of: This makes it necessary for us to refuse your request with regret.

  Say: We regret that we must, therefore, refuse your request.

Instead of: This does have a direct bearing on the possibilities for future sales.

  Say: This directly affects future sales.

Some of this wordiness stems from use of the passive; some of it comes from roundabout expressions such as *is something of vital concern,* where one verb will express the idea; and some of it results from abstract words such as *application,* which can usually be replaced by verbs.

Remember the advice of John Hookham Frere, an English diplomat and writer of the nineteenth century:

> And don't confound the language of the nation
> With long-tailed words in *osity* and *ation.*

Two things you can do to pack more action into your sentences:

1. Change words like *requirement, selection,* and *application* to verbs: *require, select,* and *apply.*
2. Use expressions such as *it is* and *there is* sparingly.

These expressions lead to such awkward and cumbersome sentences as "It is to introduce our new products that we are sending this brochure," when you can cut out the deadwood by saying "We are sending you this brochure to introduce our new products." Wordiness inevitably results in writing which overuses these expressions:

Instead of: It is my personal opinion that. . . .

  Say: I think. . . .

Instead of: There are certain problems which confront us. . . .
       Say: Certain problems confront us. . . .

Instead of: It was our understanding that. . . .
       Say: We understood that. . . .

Instead of: It is the responsibility of our Production Department
       to see that it meets the requirements of our Sales Di-
       vision. (Note that the first *it* is indefinite and the
       second refers to Production Department, making a
       very confusing sentence.)
       Say: Our Production Department must meet the require-
       ments of our Sales Division.

Be Direct

Directness results from choosing and arranging words to convey
your meaning precisely and economically. To write direct sentences,
therefore, you have to know what you want to say and how to use
words exactly. If you can't do this the first time you try, you have
to rearrange your sentences until they *are direct.*

Here's a bad example from a memorandum issued to call employees' attention to the importance of concise reports:

> Due to the fact that the production of reports involves con-
> siderable cost to our organization, it can easily be seen that the
> reduction of the time spent in writing and reading them, a shorten-
> ing of the reports themselves, would represent an appreciable gain
> in reducing our general operating expenses, although the matter
> of the length of the report should naturally be considered in rela-
> tion to the complexity of the material and its adequate coverage
> keeping in mind the necessary requirements of the specific situa-
> tion.

What, we may ask somewhat breathlessly, is this man trying to say?
Had he asked himself that, he could have decided on these three
ideas and produced two direct sentences:

> Because our reports cost money (1), we should cut the time to
> write and read them and shorten the reports (2). Their length,
> however, will depend on how complex the material is and how
> adequate the coverage ought to be for a specific situation (3).

The first step toward writing direct sentences is knowing what you want to say and then using the words which convey that meaning precisely and concisely. Notice how the changes in the following sentences improve them:

> *Wordy:* We must, therefore, keep each method of paying our salesmen a matter of information to be known only to those affected.
> *Improved:* We must, therefore, keep each method of paying our salesmen confidential.

> *Wordy:* There are changes in the organization of the department to be expected; no one as yet knows what changes will take place.
> *Improved:* No one can anticipate what changes will be made in the organization of the department.

> *Wordy:* His report discussed the risks to workers involved in leaving this equipment on our production line unguarded because this unguarded equipment increases the possibility of accidents and undermines employees' morale because of their fear of injury.
> *Improved:* He reported that unguarded equipment on our production line increased the possibility of accidents and undermined our employees' morale.

> *Wordy:* He explained that their methods of handling inquiries were antiquated and out of date and that their whole procedure of answering inquiry letters should be considered as one of the first methods of operation to be changed as soon as possible.
> *Improved:* He explained that their methods of handling inquiries were obsolete and should be changed immediately.

Keep Your Tone Appropriate

When you write, tone is particularly important. You can't convey your feeling by a smile, a gesture, or an inflection; you must rely completely on written words. And when you write in business, the tone of your writing expresses not only your own personality but that of your company. The customer who receives a discourteous, pompous, or abrupt letter may well decide that this represents the tone of the whole company. We can give so many shades of tone to our communications—positive or negative, helpful or indifferent, courteous or impertinent—that it is impossible to discuss them all. Only a highly skilled writer has complete control over the tone of his writing, but here, too, the key is understanding the reader's point of view. Here are two examples:

Please investigate this matter and *submit* a report as soon as possible.

Please *do not hesitate to* call upon us if we can be of help.

The word *submit,* which has connotations of yielding, surrendering, and showing humility, is likely to arouse resentment and hostility even though the reader may not be able to identify just what it is about the request he doesn't like. The expression *do not hesitate* suggests that the writer is so full of self-importance that he believes his reader will pause before daring to disturb him. You can improve the tone of the first sentence by substituting *let me have* or *give me* for *submit.* In the second sentence, simply delete *do not hesitate to.*

Here are two sentences from the report of an accountant on what he regarded as an improper procedure in a department of his company. Each sentence is followed by a revision written by a "writing expert." The expert believed he was improving the readability of the original without changing its meaning. Do you agree?

Mr. Smith feels there have been no violations of any company policy in his department.

Mr. Smith denies that anyone in his department has violated any company policies.

I am sure you will agree that these people's actions were not within the results we desired our policies to achieve.

I am sure you will agree that these people perverted our policies.

Test your own reactions to these sentences from letters and reports:

Since you misunderstood the proposal in our last report, the only intelligent thing to do is to abandon the project.

We do not handle inquiries from retail customers at the Central Office, but if you are still interested you can get in touch with our local dealer.

You state that your contention about a late shipment is correct, but our records do not verify your contention.

We again apologize for the dissatisfaction you had and regret our failure to correct the unfortunate error.

Be Specific

The following two paragraphs are from Merrill Lynch, Pierce, Fenner and Smith's pamphlet, *Questions and Answers about the Stock Market*. They provide a partial answer to the question "What is margin?"

When an investor or speculator with the temperament and the money to take substantial risks in the hope of substantial gains wants to increase his buying power in order to increase his stock purchases, he may decide to buy stock listed on an exchange on margin. That is, he may buy stock listed on an exchange and pay only a percentage of the cost, borrowing the rest from his broker. Here's how it works:

He decides to buy $10,000 worth of XYZ stock, but he doesn't want to use $10,000 in cash at the moment. With the margin requirement currently at 50%, he puts up $5,000, and his broker lends him the other 50%, or $5,000. The purchase must be settled promptly—within four business days at the most. He is charged the entire commission cost on the purchase of the whole $10,000 worth of stock. And he must pay monthly interest on his $5,000 loan at a rate that varies depending on the money market.

Contrast the definition of margin in the first paragraph with the illustration in the second. The definition is drab and unimpressive without the illustration. The layman, plodding through the pamphlet, probably won't remember that "he may buy stock listed on an exchange and pay only a percentage of the cost, borrowing the rest from his broker." Chances are that he *will* remember that he can buy $10,000 worth of XYZ stock, putting up $5,000 and borrowing from his broker.

It is often necessary to write in general terms; but you should remember that the further you deviate from the specific, the greater are your changes of losing your reader's interest or understanding. The business writer who says, "In this report I will attempt to analyze some of the major problems in the Alpha Window Washer company's present situation. I will give the reasons for these problems, along with my recommendations for solving them," is running an unnecessary risk. He isn't presenting a definition or a theory which has to be expressed in general terms if he has enough information on tap to be able to say:

The Alpha Window Washer company has suffered a 60 per cent decline in sales for three reasons:

1. The fierce competition offered by Beta throwaway windows
2. The 30 per cent rise in Martinis consumed by Alpha salesmen during expense account lunches
3. The high rate of loss of window washers caused by the increasing use of narrow window-ledge construction

As we have said earlier, there may be reasons for wanting to be unspecific about a given situation, but they do not include winning the attention of your reader.

5

RESEARCH METHODS

Today's business world is a world of research. And you do not need to be a scientist working in the company's laboratory to find yourself called upon to do research. Throughout the firm—in marketing, in finance, in production, in personnel administration—research increasingly forms the base for management decision making. The old-timer who operated by rule of thumb will soon be as extinct as the dodo bird.

Clearly, you will need certain skills in research methods. Some of these can only be learned after close association with the particular field of business you choose. But there are certain requirements common to all business research. We will cover some of these in this chapter.

Define Your Problem

A critical question to ask yourself as you begin to plan the research for a report—and a good one to repeat to yourself as the research progresses—is "What is the problem?"

Suppose you work for a factory manager who is plagued with complaints that special orders—orders for unusual, custom-made products—are not being completed on time. He says to you, "Find out why we can't keep track of these orders and get them out on time, and give me a report telling me what to do about it." At its broadest, your purpose or "problem" is clear: The manager wants to know how to get special orders out on time.

But you need a more specific, narrower definition of the problem before you can successfully apply research techniques to solve it. The manager implies a cause in the way he has worded his assignment: He thinks that delay is due to a failure to keep track of special orders. Is this failure then the real problem? At this point you cannot be certain. There is little doubt that special orders are not being finished on time. But the reasons why are not so clear. Could the real problem involve faulty scheduling? Or poor judgment in promising deliveries too soon? Or a system of priorities that always puts special orders after regular production? Actually, it may turn out to be a combination of these. Until you investigate a little, it is probably unwise to select any of these as *the* problem.

Suppose after some preliminary research you suspect that the main source of delay is faulty scheduling—not enough time is being allowed for some production operations, too much is allowed for others. The result is that orders are set aside at times when an operation is completed and are often not ready when an operation is supposed to begin. At this point you can begin to refine the problem definition even further. Why is the scheduling at fault? Is the "problem" carelessness among those responsible for scheduling? Are these people following a rigid policy that should be changed? Do they misunderstand the operations that must be performed and the time they take? Or do they fail to take regular production into account and, therefore, fail to plan special orders to fit into the regular production schedule? Though you are not as yet ready to fully answer these questions, you have begun to break down your original overall question into a series of questions that cover all the major alternative answers. In effect, you have a "decision tree" of possible solutions waiting for your research to fill in the facts that will finally point to the right answer or answers. Perhaps the decision tree for the problem we proposed might look like the chart on page 93. (We have carried only one segment of each line down; you would do the same for all the rest.)

In the example above we began with an overall problem in the form of an undesirable result and then proceeded to track down the source of this result in an effort to reach a more specific definition of the problem. Sometimes the reverse is called for.

Suppose you work for the vice-president in charge of production in a shoe manufacturing company. The company produces both handmade and machine-made shoes, and demand for its products has led to a need for expansion. The vice-president sees skilled hand workers as a very important part of his labor force and asks you for a report on where the company should locate a new plant in order to be assured of an adequate supply of skilled hand workers. As you try to formulate the "problem" you have been given to solve, you realize that adequacy of the supply of skilled hand workers is only a part of a larger problem: the number of hand workers actually needed. And this in turn is part of the larger problems of how big the new plant is to be and how much of its output will be handmade and how much machine-made. And these problems lead back to the problems of how fast the company wishes to grow and what balance of hand- and machine-made shoes should be planned. These problems may be beyond your jurisdiction. Some of them may be for

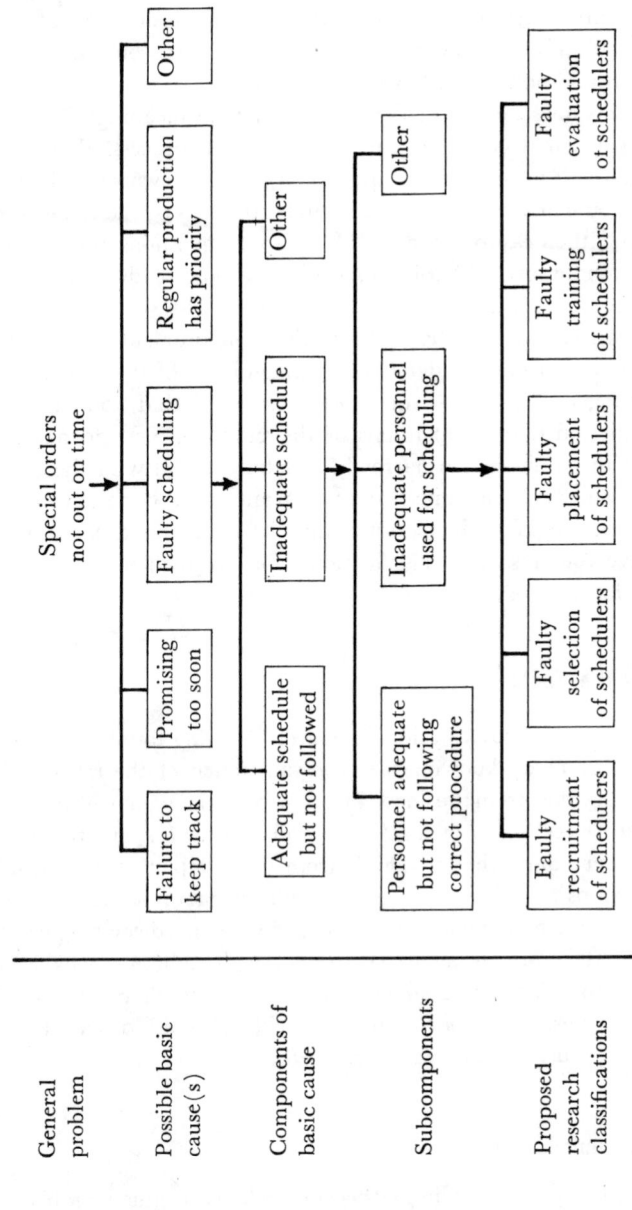

the vice-president to solve; some for the president or board of directors. Until you have solutions to these problems, you cannot solve the narrow problem you have been given.

But this does not mean that you cannot do meaningful research here. You can follow the same decision tree process, though this time you will have to move upward as well as downward. In other words, you can assume certain alternate solutions to the larger problems and then lay out the set of alternate questions that each of these assumptions calls for. Again you are now ready to fill in the empty boxes with facts.

We can summarize these observations on problem definition by saying that you must understand the magnitude of the problem you are setting out to solve—you must be satisfied that you have correctly identified the dimensions of the problem. You do not want to treat the problem too narrowly and fail to deal with the fundamental issue. At the same time, you want to be certain you have broken the main problem down into its component parts. When you have your research classifications, you are then ready to search for the facts for each.

Finding the Facts

A common difficulty in doing research is failing to take advantage of what is already known. It is true that much of the research required for reports in business involves material you get firsthand from the source—your own activities and experiences, questionnaires, work papers, and other materials from the company files, attitudes and opinions of fellow workers. We will say more about these in a moment. But, first, make certain you do not needlessly repeat research that is already available to you. Although this book is not intended to treat such sources comprehensively, there are certain important business publications that will serve as logical starting points for you. The following are useful:

Overall Guides

A helpful starting point is the comprehensive guide or bibliography of business sources. These three are examples:

DARTMOUTH COLLEGE: AMOS TUCK SCHOOL OF BUSINESS ADMINISTRATION, *A Reading List on Business Administration,* 7th rev. Hanover, New Hampshire, 1958.

HARVARD UNIVERSITY: GRADUATE SCHOOL OF BUSINESS ADMINISTRATION, BAKER LIBRARY, *Selected Reference Sources.* Boston, 1963.

H. W. JOHNSON AND S. W. MC FARLAND, *How to Use the Business Library, with Sources of Business Information.* 2d ed. Cincinnati, South-Western Publishing Company, 1957.

Indexes

There are many excellent indexes in the business field. The following are widely used:

a. *Periodical Indexes*

   Business Periodicals Index, New York: The H. W. Wilson Company (monthly, with periodic cumulations).
   Note: See *Industrial Arts Index* for articles prior to 1958.

   Public Affairs Information Service, New York: Public Affairs Information Service, Inc. (weekly, with periodic cumulations).

   Readers' Guide to Periodical Literature, New York: The H. W. Wilson Company (semimonthly, with periodic cumulations).

b. *Newspaper Indexes*

   New York Times Index (semimonthly, cumulated annually).

   Wall Street Journal Index (monthly, with annual cumulations).

Financial and Industrial Directories

These three general directories are widely used in business research:

   DUN AND BRADSTREET: *Million Dollar Directory* (annual, with supplements).
Identifies officers, products, annual sales, and numbers of employees for over 23,000 United States companies with a net worth of $1 million or more.

   Poor's Register of Corporations, Directors, and Executives of the United States and Canada (annual, with quarterly cumulated supplements).

Similar information as the above for about 29,000 corporations and for about 75,000 executives and directors.

Thomas Register of American Manufacturers (5 volumes, annual). The first three volumes list manufacturers by product, the fourth is an alphabetical directory of companies, and the fifth a "product-finding guide."

Business and Financial Periodicals

An amazing variety of periodicals are available in specialized business fields. These are also widely read for their general business information:

Barron's; National Business and Financial Weekly (weekly)

Business Week (weekly)

Commercial and Financial Chronicle (semiweekly)

Dun's Review and Modern Industry (monthly)

Fortune (monthly)

Harvard Business Review (bimonthly)

U.S. Board of Governors of the Federal Reserve System. *Federal Reserve Bulletin* (monthly)

U.S. Bureau of Labor Statistics. *Monthly Labor Review* (monthly)

U.S. Department of Commerce. *Survey of Current Business* (monthly)

Statistical Compendiums

The following contain statistics for business as a whole:

Economic Almanac. National Industrial Conference Board (annual).

Handbook of Basic Economic Statistics . . . A Manual of Basic Economic Data on Industry, Commerce, Labor, and Agriculture in the United States. Economic Statistics Bureau of Washington, D.C. (monthly, quarterly, and annually).

United Nations, Statistical Office. *Statistical Yearbook* (annual).

U.S. Bureau of the Census. *Historical Statistics of the United States.*

U.S. Bureau of the Census. *Statistical Abstract of the United States* (annual).

There are many more business sources, some of wide general interest, others of highly specialized nature. The needs of your own business will dictate the exact choices. But one overall principle remains important: Don't needlessly duplicate the search for already existing knowledge.

Gathering Firsthand Information

A large part of the research required for reports in business involves, not published material from secondary sources, but primary material you gather from your own sources. In school or college, you came much closer to the actual kind of research used in business reports if you made an investigation of such subjects as "What Students at Blank College Think about the Peace Corps" or "The Salaries and Kinds of Jobs of Last Year's Senior Class" or "A Survey of the Cost of Room and Board in Our 23 Fraternities" or "What the Student Council Should Do about Representation on the Faculty's Student Affairs Committee." To report on these subjects you needed *primary sources,* materials that were directly available on your own campus; and while you may possibly have used secondary source materials in the library—for instance, you might have compared a senior class's jobs and salaries with those of other colleges' seniors—most of your investigation should have come from facts or opinions or ideas you got firsthand. What you did if you assembled the data, information, and calculations for a laboratory report probably came closest of all in technique to the research and investigation needed for business reports, though it was probably not so polished a job as you now are expected to do.

Research that involves something other than the facilities of a library we can call *field research.* It presents some difficulties you do not encounter in *library research.* The card catalog in a library, provided you know how to use it, plus an assortment of bibliographies and indexes, will lead you to everything the library has to offer on your topic. There is no handy catalog for field research. You have to decide such things as: What information must I have? What would I like to have? What is probably available? Where? How do I go about getting it? How much will this cost? How much time will it take? How valuable will it be? And how can I implement the information—put it to work in solving my problem?

Suppose you work for the owner of a small company that is about to market a new child's toy—a small cart made to look like an automobile, in which a child can sit and propel himself by pushing pedals. The owner asks you for a report on how many carts the company can plan to sell, who will buy them, and through what distribution channels they should be sold and at what price.

As you begin to think over your problem, you may conclude that you have to know what parents would be willing to pay for the cart. It might occur to you that you would like to interview every parent within 250 miles of the company to find out. The time and expense involved would clearly be prohibitive. But suppose you took a sample of opinion. You might mail a questionnaire to a list of parents. Or you might ring some doorbells in your own city or town. Or perhaps it would be enough to ask some toy-shop owners or buyers for large stores. Or, easiest of all, you could just drop in at a toy shop or two and see what the prices are for similar products.

In order to see whether children like the toy, you might try a form of experiment—you could take two or three experimental models of the go-cart to a group of children to test their reactions as they actually drive them. The cost of this experiment may be much higher than the cost of some of the simple methods suggested earlier for obtaining price information. You might obtain some useful information from the children, but the expense incurred in gaining it might not be justified.

Which course of action you adopt will depend on how you evaluate the reliability of each course, how badly you need reliable information, how much time and money each course would involve, and how much you have to spend. It might occur to you to find out if there is a trade association for toy makers, or a magazine or journal, that may have data available on toy prices and consumer behavior. You may be able to obtain detailed information at little cost.

But, however you decide to get the information, you are going to be constantly concerned with these three criteria:

1. Is the information *valid*—are the facts the information gives accurate?
2. Is the information *reliable*—would I get the same facts if I repeated the process again at a later date?

3. Is the information applicable to my research—does it tell me something *I need to know?*

These three cardinal criteria—validity, reliability, and applicability—go far in determining what information you will choose to use in your research.

Keeping Track of Facts

The bane of the researcher is the lost fact—"I've got a note on that somewhere, but I can't put my finger on it." In anything but the simplest research the method you use to assemble your facts will go a long way toward determining whether your final product is sound. The lost fact, or the fact inadequately, or worse, inaccurately, recorded is the researcher's implacable enemy.

The first step in ensuring the defeat of this enemy is in the initial obtaining of the fact. Treat each piece of information to the famous reportorial questions "Who? When? Where? How? Why?" Be precise and accurate, even though the material you will use in business research is often not like the "hard facts" of the exact sciences. If you are interviewing a fellow worker, be certain you quote his words accurately. Be precise on his name—it would be dangerous to attribute a statement you read to Professor "Rostow," for your reader will not have you there to ask whether it was Eugene Rostow of Yale or W. W. Rostow of Harvard. (Or perhaps another Rostow altogether.) The time—and embarrassment—that you will save by being careful and exact in your gathering of facts will pay off handsomely for you. Contrariwise, slipshod research is worse than no research at all, for it dignifies inaccuracy and misinformation.

Second, you can help yourself measurably by devising a sound system of recording your information. Here accuracy and consistency will further enhance your chances of eventually being able to say exactly what you want to say in the final report.

Most likely the major part of your research can be recorded simply—in a notebook (journal) or on note cards. (As you do further research, though, you will soon become acquainted with more sophisticated techniques—punch card, electronic tape, etc.) If you choose to keep your information in a notebook or journal, you will be entering your material in a chronological or serial fashion. This has the advantage of keeping the information together in prearranged order, and you need not fear losing one item.

Though the journal has its devotees (Edward Gibbon, the famous historian was one), the use of a note card is far more widely used. Here a piece of information is entered on the card or sheet of paper (many researchers advocate only one item per card), and the cards then sorted into a scheme of classification.

In either method, though, the bywords are *system* and *consistency.* Use the top of your card or the margin of your journal for key words and phrases that allow you to classify and find information quickly. Date each piece if you use separate cards—probably at the top of the card. Be certain that you have accurate documentation. And do all these things consistently—*always* use the key words in the same way, *always* enter the date in the same place. The process will quickly become automatic for you.

Perhaps one of your note cards in the "faulty scheduling" case would look like the example on page 101.

You will soon develop further refinements that will make your own approach more able. But however you do this, remember that the important thing is to record what you need in the fashion you need it, with no lingering doubts as to the accuracy. Any worthwhile research demands just this.

Let's assume that you have followed well all the rules of data gathering and recording. Now you are ready to use these materials, though you are not yet ready for final writing. First you must apply your analytical skills to the raw data.

Fact and Opinion

Facts and opinions are the primary products of business research. It should be obvious that your facts should be relevant to your problem and that they should be complete. And, of course, your facts should be facts. High school students tend to believe that anything in print is a fact. It is to be hoped that you are beyond this. We will deal with the distinctions between facts, inferences, and assumptions after we have discussed opinions.

Opinions present more difficulty than facts do. In evaluating the usefulness of an opinion you must also consider its validity, reliability, and applicability to your research. You must ask why the source

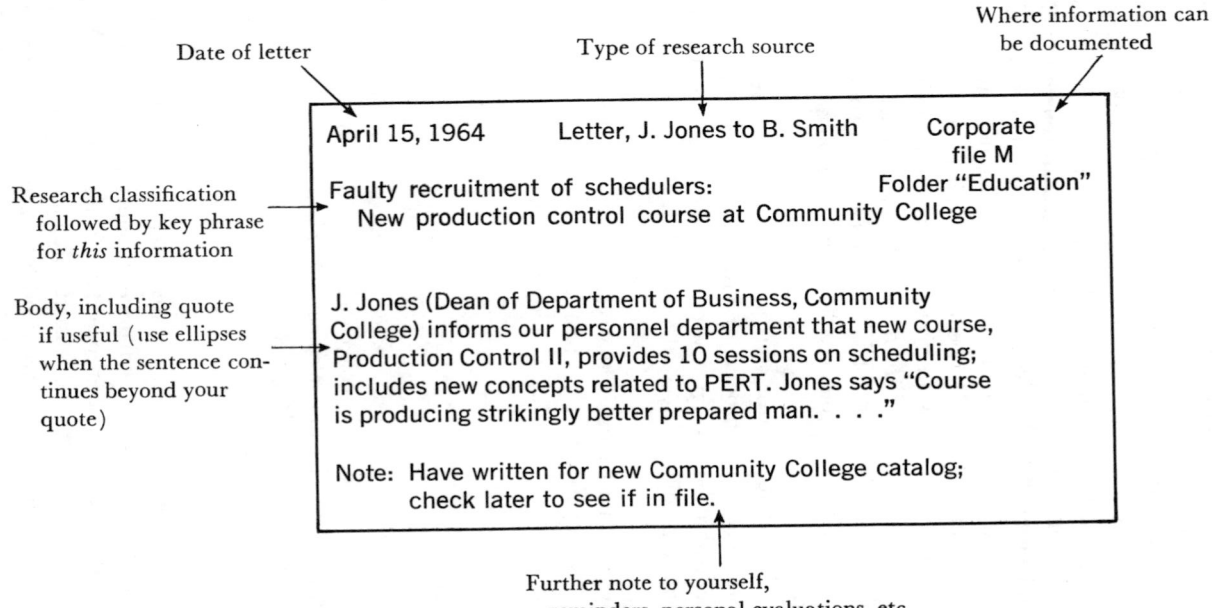

Date of letter

Type of research source

Where information can be documented

Research classification
  followed by key phrase
  for *this* information

Body, including quote
  if useful (use ellipses
  when the sentence con-
  tinues beyond your
  quote)

April 15, 1964   Letter, J. Jones to B. Smith   Corporate
                                             file M

Faulty recruitment of schedulers: Folder "Education"
  New production control course at Community College

J. Jones (Dean of Department of Business, Community
College) informs our personnel department that new course,
Production Control II, provides 10 sessions on scheduling;
includes new concepts related to PERT. Jones says "Course
is producing strikingly better prepared man. . . ."

Note: Have written for new Community College catalog;
       check later to see if in file.

Further note to yourself,
  reminders, personal evaluations, etc.

of an opinion might not be qualified or trustworthy. Has he a reputation for exaggeration or falsehood? Even if he is generally reliable, has he a personal interest he may be defending in the particular opinion he gave you? You could hardly expect the most honest sales manager to give you an unbiased opinion on whether the position of sales manager should be eliminated. You must also consider the education, experience, and general knowledge of your source in judging how well he is qualified to give an opinion. Here you may be relying on one man's opinion of the qualifications of another, and you must evaluate the first opinion to be able to evaluate the second. Of course, all such judgments are relative. There is no such thing as a perfect opinion, but some are more valid than others. You must be satisfied as to the degree of validity you need in your particular research and the degree you actually have in the opinions you have collected.

Be careful not to ignore *conflicting opinion*. It is easy to say: "I believe we can sell our product at $18.95, and six highly qualified department-store buyers agree with me," omitting the opinion of three equally qualified buyers that $14.95 is the most you should charge.

Finally, you must be sure that your source will let you use his opinion. A lot of irritation has been engendered by writers who reported the opinions of other employees without first letting them know.

Reasoning

How you reach a conclusion based on your primary product—the facts and opinions you have collected—can be described as part of a reasoning process. The four elements of this process are inference, analogy, assumption, and logic.

Inference

Suppose you observe the sales of two products, A and B, identical in all respects except name and price. Product A, which is priced below B, outsells B. In fact, in one day 10 units of A are sold for each 1 of B. So far we have discussed only facts: the nature of the products, their names, their prices, and their sales. Suppose you now conclude that A outsells B because it is cheaper. This is an inference. It is not a fact. It may be true or untrue; but until it is established as a fact or falsehood, it is an inference. Suppose that you have interviewed 600 purchasers of A and can present as a *fact* that 500 say they bought A because it was cheaper and 100 because they didn't notice B. (Notice that the reasons given are not facts, but opinions, although the *giving* of the opinions is a fact.) This information would strengthen your inference. It becomes stronger as you find more facts or opinions to support it and as you investigate and prove groundless the objections to it. But it is still not as strong as a fact.

Inferences are important, but they must be evaluated. Facts can usually, although not always, be proved without much difficulty. You can ascertain that the price of product A is $14.95, and that is that. You may be very certain of your inference that A outsells B because of its lower price, you may be fairly certain, or you may not be certain at all. When you are trying to decide whether to recommend to the manufacturer of product B that he reduce his price to increase sales, the degree of your certainty becomes important. First, you must decide whether the inference is strong enough to justify a conclusion that the price should be reduced, and second, you must explain in your report how certain you are. If your inference is little better than a guess, but you can't do any better, you should say so. Don't pretend that you are sure. Make clear to the reader of your report which conclusions you are sure of and which you are not so sure of. When he decides what to do, he will have a basis on which to evaluate the risks involved and cannot blame you for misleading him.

Many writers of business reports fail to appreciate the varying quality of inferences, and some are rather vague about the difference between fact, opinion, and inference. The result is that their analysis of a business problem is muddled and their reports do not make clear what can be relied on and what cannot, what is almost certain and what is only probable.

Here is an example of a test in which statements are classified as fact or inference, a "critical inference test." The example consists of a story, followed by a series of statements based on the story. Each statement is to be classified as factually true or false or as a strong or a weak opinion or inference. The classification is given in parentheses.

The firm of New Toys, Inc., owned by Carlton Wellman, manufactured the "Tot Walker," a device invented by Mr. Wellman to help babies learn to walk. During its first year the company sold 500 units to a large mail-order house at $3 each. The mail-order house offered them to the public at $4.50. Mr. Wellman believed the public would pay more than $4.50. He was confident that he could reduce his own price below $3 when his company began large-scale production.

1. *The "Tot Walker" was invented by Mr. Wellman.* (This is factually true, as stated in the story.)

2. *The "Tot Walker" was unique.* (This is not a fact but an inference. The story does not say whether the device was unique. We know Mr. Wellman invented it, but others may have done the same. Whether you regard the inference as trustworthy or not will depend on whether you trust Mr. Wellman to have investigated to make sure there were no similar products available.)

3. *The public will pay more than $4.50 for the device.* (This is an opinion. We are in no position to evaluate it because the story tells us nothing about Mr. Wellman's reliability or about his qualifications for judging what the public will pay for his device.)

4. *New Toys, Inc., will be able to reduce its price below $3 per unit.* (This is opinion, and not a complete opinion at that. Mr. Wellman said he could reduce the price when his company began large-scale production. If you are willing to infer that the company will begin large-scale production, then you can treat this statement as Mr. Wellman's opinion. We still have no way of judging his reliability, but he has some qualifications which lend support to this opinion. He owns the company that has been manufacturing the "Tot Walker" and he invented the product, so he could be expected to have some expert knowledge of the cost of production.)

5. *The public will pay at least $4.50 for the "Tot Walker" because 500 were sold at this price.* (This is an inference. New Toys, Inc., sold 500 to a mail-order house. We do not know how many were resold and have no way of inferring the number. There is some support for the inference that the public will pay $4.50, because it is a fact that the buyer for the mail-order house, who is presumably an expert at this sort of thing, thought they would. In other words, this inference rests on an opinion that is not expressed in the story but which we can presume.)

Analogy

Analogy is a common method of reasoning. It consists of noting that two situations are similar in several respects and concluding that the similarity will hold for other respects.

Suppose you have observed that a much-advertised brand of fresh milk sold in grocery stores consistently sells at a higher price than a less advertised brand. You reason, therefore, that an advertising campaign could enable a sugar refiner to sell its sugar for more than its competitors, who do little advertising.

The first question to ask is whether the two situations are really analogous. You have a sound analogy only if the two situations have a sufficient number of *essential characteristics in common within the area of comparison* and if there are *no essential differences* within this area.

Several similarities are evident here: Both sugar and milk are grocery items, probably purchased by the same sort of person; both are staples; both are sold in large quantities at a fairly low price per unit. These similarities are certainly within the area of comparison— importance of price. Both are white, too, but this characteristic is irrelevant. We must next ask if there is any essential difference. One such difference will probably be enough to demolish the analogy. Most people would concede that sugar is sugar; there are no noticeable differences in quality. But milk may differ in freshness and in butterfat content, within legal limits, and purchasers may detect or think they detect quality differences. If customers consider quality differences in the case of milk but not in the case of sugar, then your analogy breaks down. No matter how many similarities you can find, that one essential difference prevents you from using the results of the milk case to decide the sugar case. This doesn't prove that advertising won't enable a sugar refiner to charge more than its competitors, but it means that your milk case does not support a conclusion that it will.

Analogies, like inferences, are rarely true or false. They range from poor or weak to good or strong. And, as in the case of inferences, you must evaluate them both for yourself and for your reader.

An analogy can be dangerous if it is not tested analytically. An article in *Fortune,* entitled "The Language of Business," describes how the owners of a consumer goods corporation, who were entranced with the analogy between football and business and convinced, therefore, that building a good team was the key to success, spent all their time recruiting and training talent while their competitors developed a new product and proceeded to take away the market.

Assumption

An assumption differs from an inference. An inference is based on specific data—facts or opinions. In the example discussed above, we know that product A outsold B, we knew A was cheaper, and we knew of no other reason why purchasers would prefer A. We inferred that product A outsold product B because of its lower price. Our conclusion that purchasers would prefer a low price to a high price, however, was an *assumption*. It seemed reasonable, but we had no data to justify it. Therefore, it was not an inference. It was based on general knowledge, on experience, on what most people would call "common sense." But it was a supposition, a taking for granted, and should be recognized as such. There are instances where this particular assumption does not hold. Purchasers of jewelry, for example, or perfume, often prefer a high price to a low price because, even though they cannot perceive differences in quality, they believe that a high price in some way gives assurance of high quality.

There is nothing wrong with assumptions. We have to make them when factual data are not available and when no inferences can be drawn. In fact, we have to make assumptions about inferences. Frequently we have to assume that an inference is valid even though we are not really sure, in order to get on with research or a report. In order to discuss how large a cut in the price of product B would increase its sales to a profitable level, for example, we have to assume the validity of our inference that product A outsells it because of price. We can't set out to verify every inference as we go along. When a final conclusion is reached, however, we may want to review the inferences on which it is based and decide whether some should be verified before action is taken.

It is important not to use assumptions when data are available and inferences can be drawn. When you know the price of A is $14.95 and the price of B is $16.95, it is foolish to assume a price difference of $3. And if you have actually interviewed purchasers and found they chose A over B because of the price difference, it is not necessary to assume that some purchasers chose A because of its lower price. A conclusion that *most* purchasers will behave this way, however, may involve an assumption that your interviews are a satisfactory measure of general purchaser opinion.

It is common for a business researcher to assume that his company wants to grow as fast as possible, that a new product will add to the company's profits, or that a reduction in price will increase sales, without bothering to use data he has at hand that might lead to quite opposite inferences. It is, unfortunately, always easier to assume than to work with data and infer.

Assumptions, like inferences and analogies, must be evaluated. An assumption must be consistent with the available data; it must have a reasonable possibility of being true. You can't assume no one will buy product B at a price of $16.95 when you know perfectly well that people are buying it.

It is especially important to label your assumptions. Be honest enough with the reader of your reports to tell him when you have no data and are relying on assumption or when you are not certain of the validity of an inference but will assume it is valid for purposes of further discussion. Your reader may disagree with your assumptions: He may feel his experience and general knowledge are a better guide than yours. At the same time, he may respect your inferences as being based on a familiarity with the data greater than his own. Give him the opportunity to sort out the assumptions from the inferences.

When you have completed a research project and reached a conclusion, it is important to review the inferences, analogies, and assumptions that went into it. You must judge the *importance* and the *validity* of each one. When you write your report, perform the same service for your reader. That is, identify the important inferences, analogies, and assumptions. Assure him of their relative validity, which means also warning him of unavoidable weaknesses. And point out which are less important, so he won't expect detailed evaluation of these.

Logic

There should be no need to stress the importance of logic in business research and business writing. Yet business reports all too frequently reveal the writer's failure to test his statements on logical grounds.

An example is quoted below. It is taken from a report on the subsidizing of scholarly books published by a university press. Subsidized books are not expected to sell well enough to reimburse the publisher for their cost. Sometimes the publisher expects to lose money on a book, and hence to subsidize it; sometimes other institutions—educational foundations or councils—will provide the funds (a collateral subsidy) to make publication possible. It is often argued that if a foundation provides the money to subsidize a scholarly book which later proves to be profitable, the university press should refund the subsidy. The following paragraph from the report deals with this argument.

It is occasionally suggested that a collateral subsidy should be "returnable," that is, that when the Press has recovered all its costs of publication, further proceeds, if any, should be applied to the reduction of the investment of the institution which provided the collateral subsidy. At first sight, this suggestion may seem to have merit, but in practice serious flaws appear. First, it will be noted that such a grant is not a genuine subsidy, but simply the provision of working capital, which may or may not be needed. Secondly, if the Press does not recover from sales its costs of publication above the amount of the collateral subsidy, its funds will be depleted—it is therefore risking an indefinite sum on its publishing judgment, and it should not speculate with the Subsidizing Fund on the basis that it will either be depleted or exactly reimbursed. Thirdly, the administrative cost of recording, computing, and returning proceeds in very small amounts is disproportionately high, and could even exceed possible returns. The situation is quite different if the institution providing the subsidy underwrites the entire cost; it is then assuming the whole publishing risk, and is entitled to all proceeds over and above the actual cost of handling sales.

Let us look at the three "serious flaws." The first argument is that if a grant is repaid it is not a genuine subsidy. This is not a logical argument; it is a play on words. *Subsidy* is defined in Webster's dictionary as "any gift by way of financial aid." If the gift is returned, it is perhaps no longer a gift. But it really makes no difference to the foundation whether this money is called a gift, subsidy, or refundable advance.

We can break the second argument down into three parts. First, the writer says that if the press does not recover its own costs of publication over the amount of the subsidy, its funds will be depleted. But this argument is fallacious, since the writer has already stated at the beginning of his paragraph that the suggestion he is disputing is that the collateral subsidy be repaid only after the press has recovered all its costs of publication.

The second portion of the second argument is that the press would be risking an indefinite sum on its publishing judgment if it returned a gift from another institution once a book had recovered its cost. It is hard to tell what the writer had in mind here. The risk was run when the book was published, when no one knew whether it would sell enough copies to repay its cost. Returning the gift after the book proved profitable could not increase this risk. Even so, the risk was never an indefinite one. The press knew how much money it was putting up to publish the book, and it knew that at most it could lose this amount.

The third portion of the second argument is that the press should not speculate with the funds available for subsidizing books in the expectation that these funds will be either depleted or exactly reimbursed. In other words, subsidizing funds should be used only when there is also a possibility of making money on a scholarly book. But the original suggestion seemed to be that a foundation's subsidy be returned to it only *after* the press had recovered all its costs and that *only* the subsidy be returned, so that any profit would be kept by the press. Thus the statement that the result could only be depletion of funds or exact reimbursement is false. (It may be that the writer meant to discuss a suggestion that profits would go to the foundation; the first sentence in the paragraph quoted is ambiguous.)

The third argument may have some merit, but the amount of bookkeeping involved would probably be no greater than is always necessary in order to compute an author's royalty.

The quoted example is an interesting one because, on superficial reading, it appears to make sense. You have to subject each of the writer's arguments to rather close scrutiny to discover that, on a logical basis, it falls apart.

This chapter cannot offer you a course in logic. But we have already discussed the use and misuse of inferences, analogies, and assumptions, and we will deal briefly with two classes of fallacious reasoning because they are so common in business reports. These are *begging the question* and the *non sequitur*.

Begging the Question

When a writer begs the question, he assumes what must be proven and, therefore, simply substitutes one question for another. Here is an example:

> I have no hesitation in recommending this investment because the return on it will be more than satisfactory.

In this sentence, the writer is *assuming* a satisfactory return in order to support a recommendation for investment. Whether the return will be satisfactory is the key question, the one that must be answered affirmatively before the recommendation can be justified. In other words, the question "Should I invest?" is not very different from "Will the return be satisfactory?" and you cannot logically answer the first by assuming an answer to the second. What the example above really says is "I assume the investment should be made because I assume the return will be more than satisfactory." The recommendation is now shown for what it really is: a pure assumption, not a logical inference.

Non Sequitur

Non sequitur, which means "it does not follow," is perhaps the most common fallacy in business reports. In a strict sense, every inference that is not justified by the data from which it is drawn is a *non sequitur*. The *non sequiturs* with which we are particularly concerned are conclusions drawn from irrelevant or quite insufficient data. For example:

> There are several communities within a 50-mile radius of our plant where we do not have stores. Most of our business is done with local customers; therefore, I believe that any stores opened in these towns would increase customers and sales.

The fact that most business is done with local, as opposed to non-local, customers does not justify the stated conclusion. The writer may have had some reason to think his premise was relevant to his conclusion, but he has not given it to us. Here is another example:

> We are just breaking even at our present sales volume. Because of competition we cannot raise our prices; therefore, the only other way to make a profit is to lower costs.

The writer is concluding that there are only two ways to make a profit —raise prices or lower costs. And he deduces this, or appears to, from the fact that the company is breaking even. The conclusion simply does not follow. Why, for example, is an increase in sales volume not a way to make a profit?

If our discussion of reasoning and logic points to one thing, it is the need for care—for a study of every inference, analogy, assumption, and conclusion, to make sure that it makes sense logically.

A Concluding Word on Research

As you finally write your research report, you will be using, hopefully, both the ideas in this chapter and those in the rest of the book. Clear and simple writing, based on careful organization, are the keynotes of business research reports just as in other business writing. But it is still true that, as important as is the "How you say it," the "What you say" is the basis for final judgment. What was the problem you set out to solve? Did you solve it? Put another way, did you provide dependable and accurate material which your original questioner can now use as he begins to implement his plans? This can only be true if you have been careful and authoritative in the research methods described in this chapter. You may find the following summary helpful in remembering and applying them.

1. **Defining the Problem**

   Have I isolated the fundamental problem facing me? Am I dealing with a problem that can only be solved by making certain assumptions about other problems? Have I broken down my problem into its component parts, so that I can begin to organize the research needed to solve the problem?

2. **Finding the Facts**

   What information is necessary? Not necessary, though possibly desirable? Where can I obtain it? How difficult will this be? Am I wasting my energies searching for already known facts? Will the information be worth its cost? Is the information I find *valid, reliable,* and *applicable?*

3. **Keeping Track of Facts**

   Is my system of recording accurate and consistent? Have I documented adequately?

4. **Fact and Opinion**

   Have I clearly differentiated between what is fact and what is opinion? Have I judged the reliability and qualifications of the sources of opinions I am relying on? Can I convince my reader of the value of these opinions?

5. **Inference**

   What is the basis for the inferences I have drawn? How reliable are these inferences? How important are they to my conclusions? And have I always alerted my reader to my judgments as to the accuracy and reliability of my inferences?

6. **Analogy**

   When I draw an analogy, am I comparing things that are *essentially* the same? Have I overlooked any essential difference? Have I used analogy only when it usefully applies?

7. **Assumption**

   Are my assumptions necessary? Have I exhausted my resources of fact and inference? How reliable are my assumptions, and how important are they? Have I clearly identified for my reader the assumptions I have made, and have I shown him their reliability and importance?

8. **Begging the Question**

   Have I pretended to reach a conclusion by logic when really I have simply assumed the conclusion?

9. **Non Sequitur**

   Do my conclusions really follow from my reasoning? When I describe or imply a cause-and-effect relationship, does this relationship really exist?

10. **Did I Solve the Problem?**

    Or did I give my reader the material necessary for him to solve it?

6

STATISTICS IN BUSINESS RESEARCH

Within the confines of a single chapter it is impossible to deal with statistics in detail. What we will do in this chapter is provide three services for the reader. We will present the basic concepts of descriptive statistics, discussing them in nonmathematical terms. We will explain one of the most useful statistical devices—multiple regression—without any mathematics beyond simple arithmetic. And finally, we will discuss briefly statistical decision making, including the use of the new, so-called "Bayesian" [1] statistics.

Descriptive statistics, as the name suggests, is concerned with statistical devices useful in representing relationships among data. Perhaps the simplest of these devices is the frequency distribution.

Frequency Distribution

Suppose we have 9 employees, aged 19, 23, 23, 25, 27, 34, 34, 34, and 78. In order to get a picture of this age pattern, we could plot a frequency distribution. One method is illustrated in Figure 6-1.

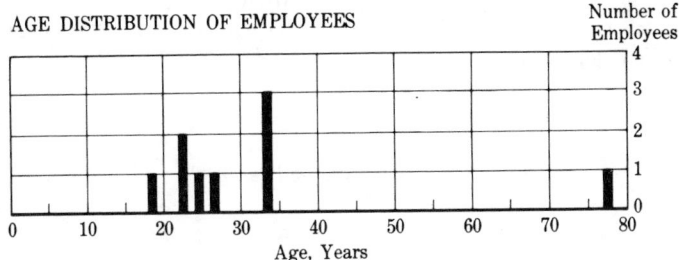

Figure 6-1

In this graph the horizontal axis is marked off by ages and the vertical axis is marked off by numbers of employees of each age. From our graph we can get some notion of the age structure of our employee group; the graph presents dramatically the numerical data we assembled.

We can also derive a single numerical characteristic of the age structure of the group. One such number is the average.

[1] The name "Bayesian" comes from the Rev. Thomas Bayes (1702–1761), a famous English mathematician.

Average

The average, or more technically, the "arithmetic mean," of a series of measurements is the sum of the measurements divided by the number of measurements. In the case of our example above, the average is $(19 + 23 + 23 + 25 + 27 + 34 + 34 + 34 + 78)/9 = 297/9$, or 33 years.

A "weighted" average is an average deduced by giving different relative importance to different measurements. We could have used a weighted average to compute the average of 33 above. The employees fall into 6 age brackets: 19, 23, 25, 27, 34, and 78. An average of these 6 ages will not give us the average age of the employees because, for example, there are 3 employees aged 34 and only 1 aged 19. But if we weight these 6 ages appropriately in computing the average, we will arrive at the correct average age for the group. We simply weight each of the ages by the number of employees of that age and multiply each age by its weight. We add the results of these multiplications and divide by the sum of the weights, not the number of ages, to get the true average. Table 6-1 shows the calculations.

Table 6-1

Age	Weight	Age $\times$ Weight
19	1	19
23	2	46
25	1	25
27	1	27
34	3	102
78	1	78
Total	9	297

Average: $297/9 = 33$

The average is in one respect more convenient to record as a characteristic of the age pattern than was the frequency distribution: It is a single number rather than a whole set of numbers or a graph. But in gaining a single measure we have lost some information. Many sets of numbers have the same average but quite different distributions, and the average tells us nothing about the distribution. The average is useful in various ways, however. For example, it may be of help in determining the cost of a pension plan for the employees. For other purposes the average should be complemented by the median.

Median

The median is the value that lies midway in a series of measurements. In our example, the median age of the employees is 27—as many employees are younger than 27 as are older. If we had eight employees, the median would lie between the ages of the fourth and fifth oldest, and the usual rule of thumb is to select the age midway between the ages of these two.

If we want to get a feel for whether our employees are a "young group" or an "old group," the median will be a better guide than the average. The average is heavily affected by the age of the 78-year-old. Apart from him, the employees are actually rather young, and the median, in telling us that half the employees are under 27, gives us a better picture of the make-up of the group.

Of course, the frequency distribution we plotted in Figure 6-1 gives us an even better picture than the median does. But the median, like the average, offers the convenience of a single number to work with. Notice that the median and average together tell us something about the form of the frequency distribution. Since the median is below the average, we know the distribution is "skewed" toward higher ages. That is, the distribution is not symmetrical; there are more employees toward the low-age end of the distribution than toward the high-age end.

Another example may point up more clearly the difference between the usefulness of the average and that of the median. Suppose we want to establish what kind of customers patronize a retail grocery store, and as a part of this project we are interested in establishing the "typical" size of purchase. Suppose further that over a given day the average purchase (the day's sales divided by the number of purchases) is $15, while the median purchase is only $6.50. The distribution is again skewed, with purchases bunched at the low end of the scale. We know that half the purchases were for less than $6.50 and half were for more. Because the average is $15, we can conclude there were some very large market baskets that day. But it seems reasonable to conclude that most of the purchases were close to $6.50.

When the average and the median are far apart, we know that the distribution is skewed. We may also be interested in knowing how "spread out" our data are. A degree of "spread" is measured by the standard deviation.

Standard Deviation

It may be hard to see why we should be concerned about the spread in the examples we have been using. But suppose what we are measuring is the size of holes drilled in steel plates by an automatic drilling machine and that we know the holes must be 1.125 inches in diameter, plus or minus 0.002 inch. If we measure a sample of drilled holes and discover the average diameter to be 1.124 inches, we know that *on the average* the machine is drilling holes that are slightly small but still within acceptable limits. It may be time to make adjustments, to replace a worn bit, for example, in order to bring the size closer to standard. But if we also discovered a wide spread in the measurements, we would be much more concerned—there would be more wrong with the machine than a worn bit.

The standard deviation is a device we use to measure the spread in a series of measurements. It is defined as the square root of the average of the squares of the deviations of the measurements from the average measurement. In our example of 9 employees, the deviations from the average age of 33 are 14, 10, 10, 8, 6, 1, 1, 1, and 45. The squares of these numbers are 196, 100, 100, 64, 36, 1, 1, 1, and 2,025. The sum of these is 2,588, the average is roughly 288, and the square root of this average is about 17. This is the standard deviation.

The less spread out the measurements are, the smaller the standard deviation will be. (Obviously if there is no spread at all, the standard deviation will be zero.) From Figure 6-1 we can see that if the employee group did not include the 78-year-old, the ages would be much less spread out, and in fact the standard deviation would be only 5.5.

The standard deviation has properties that make it an important measure of spread. And the standard deviation is quite useful when we are dealing with data that are "normally distributed."

Normal Distribution

We began this discussion by talking about frequency distribution. A normal distribution is a frequency distribution with special properties. To explain the properties would involve a long digression into mathematics, but we can at least describe some of the characteristics of a normal distribution. Imagine the bars in Figure 6-1 greatly reduced in width and increased in number, until the graph takes the form of a solid area bounded on the top by a smooth curve. If the distribution were normal, the curve would be bell-shaped; it would be symmetrical about a vertical line through its center; it would extend to infinity in both directions along the horizontal axis, but it would come very close to the axis not far from its center.

The true normal distribution is an ideal never quite attained in the real world. But often we find business data form distributions close enough to normal distributions that we can treat the data as though they were normally distributed. For example, suppose we made a great many measurements of diameters of holes drilled in bar stock by an automatic drilling machine. We would not expect the holes to be absolutely identical. The machine is not perfect; many parts of it will have small irregularities. The bar stock will not be perfectly homogeneous. And there will probably be vibrations from the machine's surroundings affecting its output, as well as minor variations in the power supplied to the machine. Since deviations from the average size of the drilled holes will be the result of a great variety of minor irregularities, working more or less at random, we would expect the frequency distribution of sizes of holes to be nearly normal. We would certainly expect few of the holes to be very far from the average and quite a few to be slightly off average, and we would expect symmetry: We would expect to find as many undersized as oversized holes. We know the distribution cannot be exactly normal, because, for one thing, we cannot have holes of negative size, and a normal distribution must extend to minus infinity and to plus infinity.

It is useful to approximate a frequency distribution to a normal distribution because a very large body of statistical theory has been developed to deal with normal distributions, and it is helpful to be able to use this theory. One property of a normal distribution is that about 68 per cent of the data will lie within the standard deviation from the average, 95 per cent will lie within twice the standard deviation, and 99.7 per cent will lie within three times the standard deviation.

Index Numbers

Index numbers, particularly those computed and published by government agencies, have become very popular among business researchers, especially for reporting and summarizing data. An index number is usually a weighted average, made up of a variety of components combined in certain proportions, designed to characterize some important process. For example, the Consumer Price Index published by the Bureau of Labor Statistics measures the average change in the price of a "package" of about four hundred goods and services, combined in proportions that the Bureau believes represented the typical 1960–1961 spending pattern for city wage earners and clerical workers. The validity of the index depends, of course, on the validity of the judgment that went into the selections of the goods and services to be included and the choice of their proportions, as well as on the accuracy of measurement, from month to month, of the prices of each of these goods and services. The usefulness of the index generally will depend upon these factors as well as on whether patterns of spending have changed so that the 1960–1961 "package" is no longer typical. It is interesting that until 1964 this index was based on a 1951–1952 "package," which gave more emphasis to food and less to housing and transportation than the new index does.

The usefulness of the Consumer Price Index to any particular business researcher will depend, of course, upon whether this index has any relevance to the characteristic of his business that he is measuring. We will discuss this relevance in quantitative terms below, under Multiple Regression.

As we noted above, an index measures an average "change," and it is important to keep the change in mind. An index will be arbitrarily set at 100 for a "base period." In the case of the Consumer Price Index the base period is 1957–1959. The index for any other period then measures the change from the base period. A Consumer Price Index of 107.7 for March, 1964, means that the "package" of goods and services cost 107.7 per cent in March, 1964, of what its average cost was in 1957–1959. And it records a small upward movement in prices since February, 1964, when the index was 107.6 per cent. Note that what the user of the index is interested in is not the particular price of the "package" in any given month or year, but whether the price is rising or falling, and, in percentage terms, by how much.

Multiple Regression

Of all the statistical tools available to the businessman, regression analysis is perhaps the most valuable. It is also one of the simplest to use, at least with graphic methods. These are less precise than mathematical methods but still quite adequate for most business purposes. We are going to discuss a business problem, explore some statistical measurements that may be helpful in solving it, and carry out a regression analysis.

Our problem is to forecast the sales of a product, and we begin with sales data for the past ten years, shown in Table 6-2.

Table 6-2

Year	1	2	3	4	5	6	7	8	9	10
Unit sales (thousands)	92.8	92.5	92.5	92.0	92.1	90.9	90.9	91.1	90.7	90.0

What can we do with these figures? For one thing, we might compute their arithmetical average. This is 91.5. We could estimate the eleventh year's sales at 91.5 simply because, on the average, this is what sales have been over the past ten years. This does not seem a very good method, because for one thing, it takes no account of whether sales have been improving, worsening, or staying level. To see what has been happening over the ten-year period, we can draw a graph of sales. This is shown in Figure 6-2.

Figure 6-2 suggests that sales have been following a fairly steady downward trend. We might try to draw a line—a "trend line"—to represent this trend. What we want is the "best straight line" we can draw through the points on the graph. We could use a curved trend

UNIT SALES BY YEARS

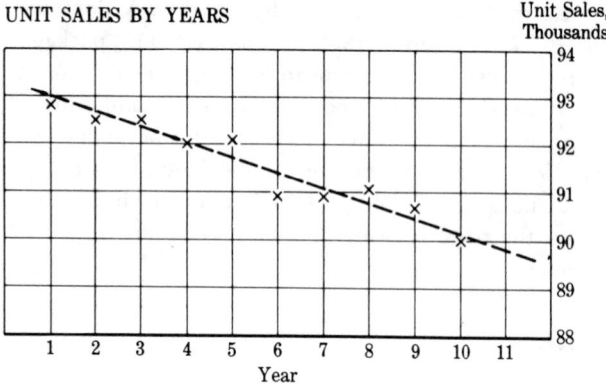

Figure 6-2

line, but if the points seem to lie fairly close to a straight line, it is sufficient to draw a straight line. Handling regression based on straight-line relationships is much easier than handling curved relationships, although the latter is not impossible. A best straight line is simply a line that seems to best represent the trend of sales from year to year. In theory, it should be placed so that the sum of the squares of the distances of the points from the line is a minimum. If you are willing to take the trouble, you can determine the vertical distance of each point on the graph from the line you have drawn, square these distances, and add the squares. Then shift the line, measure the new distances, and find a new sum of the squares. The line that gives the smaller sum is the better one, and the process can be repeated as long as you like. This is the "least-squares" method of finding the best straight line, and as you might suspect, there are mathematical devices for determining where the line should go without the need for trial-and-error drawing. But for most purposes you will find trial and error satisfactory.

If you are curious about why the least-squares method works, recall our calculation of the standard deviation—the square root of the average of the squares of the deviations of each measurement from the average. We would like the "spread" of the points from the line to be as small as possible; hence we want the square root of the average of the squares of the distances of the points from the line to be as small as possible, which means we want the sum of the squares to be small.

A trend line is shown in Figure 6-2 (as a broken line). It suggests that sales for the eleventh year will be about 89.8. But at this point we should stop and realize that we have so far completely ignored the factors that *cause* sales to follow a certain trend and the possibility of predicting these factors and from them predicting sales.

In searching for factors influencing sales, one obvious consideration is price. In Table 6-3 we have a tabulation of both unit sales

Table 6-3

Year	Unit sales (thousands)	Price ($ per unit)
1	92.8	$ 7.80
2	92.5	7.90
3	92.5	7.45
4	92.0	8.45
5	92.1	7.75
6	90.9	8.80
7	90.9	8.80
8	91.1	8.95
9	90.7	8.75
10	90.0	8.50
Average	91.5	8.32

and unit price for the past ten years. What can we do with these new figures? For one thing, we can confirm in a rather rough way from inspection that, in general, when the price was increased sales dropped and when the price fell sales rose. This is about what we might have expected. But even this relationship holds for only the first seven years, and unless we can find some quantitative relationship (how *much* do sales rise when price is reduced a given amount?), it will be hard to use the price-sales relationship from the past to predict future sales. Again, a graph may help us. In Figure 6-3 are plotted unit sales and unit price. Each cross represents sales and price for one of the ten years, and the crosses are numbered to indicate which year's data are represented. The heavy black dot represents the average unit sales (91.5) and the average price ($8.32) for the ten-year period. The picture presented by the scattering of crosses is about what we expected: The higher the price,

UNIT SALES BY PRICE

Unit Sales,
Thousands

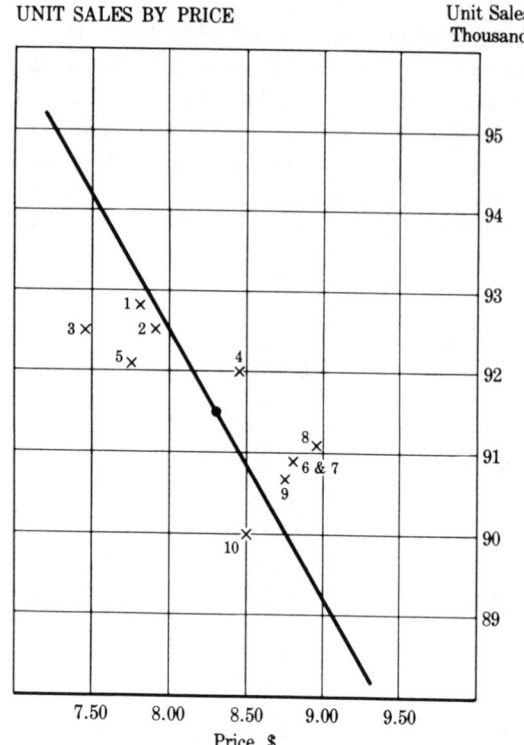

Price, $

Figure 6-3

in general, the lower the unit sales. But we are looking for a more precise relationship, so we draw the best straight line we can through the scattering of crosses, making sure the line passes through the black dot representing the average sales and price. We could use a curved line instead of a straight line, but as we noted above, the straight line is adequate.

The line we have drawn is a "regression" line. It shows the way unit sales behave with price and gives us a basis for predicting sales if we know the price. For example, if the price in the eleventh year is to be $8.75, we would predict sales at 90.0.

We have improved our ability to forecast by considering price and discovering the regression of sales on price. But the regression is not entirely satisfactory. The crosses in Figure 6-3 are rather widely scattered, and it seems unwise to put too much faith in the best straight line as a true measure of how sales are related to price. This is not surprising. Sales of most goods are affected by more factors than just price changes. One such important factor may be advertising. Table 6-4 adds a record of advertising expenditure to the data given in Table 6-3.

Table 6-4

Year	Unit sales (thousands)	Price ($ per unit)	Advertising ($ thousands)
1	92.8	7.80	66.6
2	92.5	7.90	68.3
3	92.5	7.45	65.4
4	92.0	8.45	68.5
5	92.1	7.75	66.0
6	90.9	8.80	70.2
7	90.9	8.80	71.9
8	91.1	8.95	75.2
9	90.7	8.75	68.3
10	90.0	8.50	64.0
Average	91.5	8.32	68.4

With the aid of Table 6-4 we can begin to find some explanation for the scatter of the crosses in Figure 6-3. In years 3 and 5, for example, when unit sales seemed rather low considering the price that was in effect, advertising was below average. And in years 6, 7, and 8, when unit sales seemed high considering the price, advertising was above average. The important question is "*How much* difference did advertising make?" If we are to predict sales on the basis of advertising information, we must have a numerical relationship, just as we established such a relationship between sales and price with the straight line in Figure 6-3.

Our next step is to find the exact amount by which our straight line in Figure 6-3 deviates from the actual sales data and to correlate this with advertising. To begin with, we tabulate the sales figures for each of the ten years that the straight line in Figure 6-3 would lead us to expect. In other words, for each year, we record not the actual sales but the sales shown by the straight line. These are listed in column (5) of Table 6-5, and in order to reduce the repetition of tabular data, we will add some other columns to Table

Table 6-5

Year	Unit sales (thousands)	Price ($ per unit)	Advertising ($ thousands)	Expected sales (from Fig. 6-3)	Actual sales less expected sales	Expected change due to adv. (from Fig. 6-4)	Expected sales based on price and adv. data
(1)	(2)	(3)	(4)	(5)	(6)	(7)	(8)
1	92.8	7.80	66.6	93.2	−0.4	−0.5	92.7
2	92.5	7.90	68.3	92.9	−0.4	−0.1	92.8
3	92.5	7.45	65.4	94.2	−1.7	−1.0	93.2
4	92.0	8.45	68.5	91.0	1.0	0	91.0
5	92.1	7.75	66.0	93.3	−1.2	−0.8	92.5
6	90.9	8.80	70.2	89.9	1.0	0.6	90.5
7	90.9	8.80	71.9	89.9	1.0	1.0	90.9
8	91.1	8.95	75.2	89.3	1.8	2.2	91.5
9	90.7	8.75	68.3	90.0	0.7	0	90.0
10	90.0	8.50	64.0	90.9	−0.9	−1.4	89.5
Average	91.5	8.32	68.4				

6-5 which are not discussed until later. Next we compute the amount by which our best straight line in Figure 6-3 differs from the actual sales data. This is the difference between the figures in column (2), the actual sales figures, and those in column (5). These differences we record in column (6). Next we plot the figures in column (6) against advertising expenditures, as shown in Figure 6-4. Figure 6-4 shows us the relationship between the "error," if it can be called that, of our line in Figure 6-3 and advertising. In other words, it shows how well the deviation of the expected sales figures from the actual sales figures, given the price, is explained by changes in advertising expenditures. The explanation is fairly good; the crosses in Figure 6-4 lie fairly close to a straight line. We draw again a best straight line, passing through the black spot representing the average advertising expenditure and zero deviation of actual sales from expected sales. Again we have a regression line, one that we can use to try to predict sales.

DIFFERENCE BETWEEN ACTUAL
SALES AND SALES EXPECTED ON THE
BASIS OF FIGURE 6-3 BY ADVERTISING

Difference
in Thousands
of Units

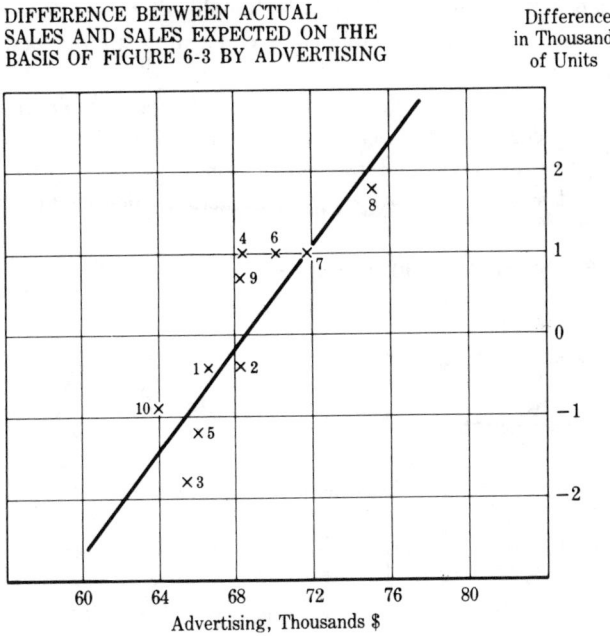

Advertising, Thousands $

Figure 6-4

Our prediction method is now a little more complicated than it was when we had only a regression line connecting price with sales. Given a price and a figure for advertising expenditure, we deduce a sales figure now, using both Figures 6-3 and 6-4. For example, if the price is to be $8.25 and advertising is to be 72.0, we first conclude from Figure 6-3 that sales will be 91.7, before allowing for the fact that advertising will be above the average. Then from Figure 6-4 we read off 1.2 as the amount that must be added to the 91.7 to allow for advertising. Our forecast is then sales of 92.9.

Strictly speaking, what we have done is only an approximate multiple regression. Theoretically, we should draw our best straight lines in Figures 6-3 and 6-4 simultaneously. The point is that a line that is not quite the best straight line in Figure 6-3 might produce a very good line-up of points in Figure 6-4, and what we want is the best pair of straight lines. As long as we are using graphical methods there is nothing we can do about this. We have to draw the line in Figure 6-3 before we can plot Figure 6-4. There are mathematical methods that will simultaneously handle all three of the sales, price, and advertising variables and come up with the best overall regression.

How good is our method now? Just as Figure 6-3 gave us a picture of how good the correlation is between sales and price, Figure 6-5 gives us a picture of how good the correlation is between price, advertising, and sales. The crosses represent actual sales (column

ACTUAL AND PREDICTED SALES BY YEARS

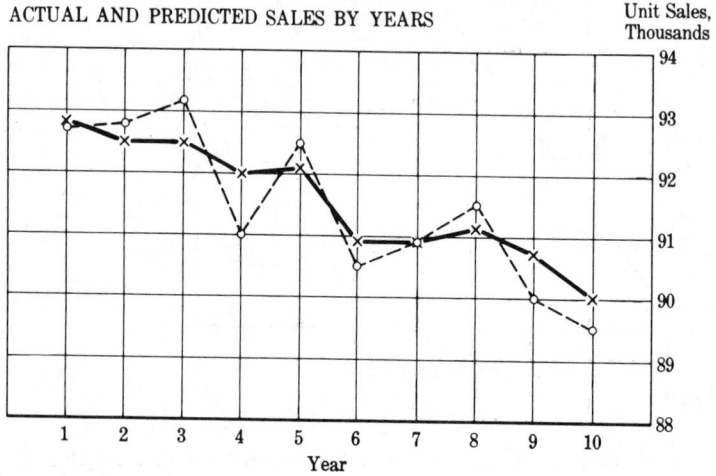

Figure 6-5

(2) in Table 6-5), plotted for each year. The zeros represent the sales figures we would have predicted on the basis of Figures 6-3 and 6-4, given the price and advertising information (columns (3) and (4) in Table 6-5). These expected sales figures are calculated as explained in the preceding paragraph and are tabulated in column (8) of Table 6-5.

Whether the correlation shown by Figure 6-5 is good enough for your purposes will depend upon your own demands for precision. If you are not satisfied, you can go on to consider more variables. You might, for example, consider prices of competitive products. Or you might make fuller use of the data we already have. Figure 6-2 suggests that time itself is a variable that can be used to predict sales. That is really what we concluded when we drew a trend line. You could measure the deviation of each point on Figure 6-2 from the trend line and then plot these deviations against price, just as we plotted deviations against advertising expenditures in Figure 6-4. Then you could measure the deviations of the points on this new graph from the best straight line and plot these deviations against advertising expenditures, again drawing in a best straight line. Now the forecasting will involve three instead of two calculations.

There is a danger in continuing to add variables. If you add enough variables, you can come up with perfect regression: You will get a regression line that fits the data exactly. And this is true even if the variables could not possibly have anything to do with sales. The diagrams will help to tell you whether the variables you have chosen are relevant. If a variable is relevant, the crosses should lie on a fairly smooth line (not necessarily a straight line but a smooth one). If it is minor you will probably find no pattern to the diagram. But of course a lack of pattern may just indicate that two or more factors are important and they tend to obscure one another. You must depend heavily, then, on your own judgment of what is important and what is not.

It would be clear that there is no "magic" in multiple regression. Even if Figure 6-5 demonstrated a perfect fit of our calculated sales with actual sales for the past ten years, if the price-advertising-sales relationship should change in the eleventh year, then the data we have assembled for forecasting will not work. What the technique does is to offer a device for assembling and handling data. Its results can be no better than the researcher's judgment.

Statistical Decision Making

What we have discussed so far is descriptive statistics—devices for summarizing data and discovering relationships. We end the chapter with a brief introduction to the use of statistics in decision making. The limitations of space and a determination to avoid mathematics present even more difficulty here than in the section on descriptive statistics, and the discussion will therefore be even more general. Its purpose is to give some idea of the kinds of problems statistics can be used to solve, and how these problems are solved. Here we make special reference to the difference between classical and so-called Bayesian statistics.

Suppose our company is purchasing parts, in batches, to be used in a production process. We know from experience that in each of these batches there will be some defective parts. We can allow a batch to go into the production process, where the defectives will sooner or later be found and discarded. Or we can examine all the parts in a batch and discard the defectives *before* they reach the production process. If there are few defectives in a batch, the inconvenience of discovering them in the course of the production process may not be very great and we may prefer not to go to the trouble of examining every part. That is, we may prefer to "accept" rather than to "screen." But if there is a high proportion of defectives in a batch, the inconvenience of discovering them in the production process may be very great, and in this case we would rather screen the batch. If we knew exactly how many defectives there were in a given batch, it would be relatively easy to decide whether to accept or to screen the batch, but in practice we do not know. A sampling plan might help us.

We can take a sample of parts from a batch and examine each part in the sample for less than it would cost us to examine every part in the batch, that is, for less than it would cost us to screen the batch. Of course, the sample will not tell us with certainty how many defectives there are in the batch. A batch of 100 parts may contain 10 defectives, and a sample of 10 parts from the batch might contain all the defectives. But the probabilities are that the sample will give a reasonable indication of the percentage of defectives in the batch. Of course, the bigger the sample, the greater the chance it will give us a percentage as close as we want to the correct percentage of defectives, but the bigger the sample, the more it costs to sample. In sampling we strike a compromise between accuracy of information and the cost of obtaining it.

What we would like is a sampling plan that will tell us to screen the batches with high proportions of defectives and accept those with low proportions. We might note here that a sampling plan is characterized by two numbers: the number of parts to be taken from the batch—the "sample size"—and the percentage of defectives in the sample that will serve as a signal to screen or accept. If the percentage of defectives in the sample is above this latter number, we will screen the batch; if it is equal to or below it, we will accept.

The sampling plan will not be perfect. Sometimes it will indicate that the percentage of defectives in a batch is low, and we will not screen, and the batch will turn out to have a high percentage of defectives and we may wish we had screened. But the sampling plan will enable us to make better decisions whether or not to screen than we could make without it. Our problem is to discover the best sampling plan.

First we will discuss the classical method for finding the plan. We want a plan that will lead us to screen batches with high proportions of defectives and not to screen batches with low proportions, and we know that no plan will give us perfect advice. Now we have to be more specific, and put this objective in numerical terms. We might decide that if a batch has only 5 per cent defectives we want our plan to offer us a probability of 80 per cent that we will accept, and if the batch has 10 per cent defectives we want the plan to offer us a probability of 75 per cent that we will screen. In other words, we want to be able to expect that eighty times out of a hundred when we sample batches containing 5 per cent defectives, the sample plan will signal us to accept, and that seventy-five times out of a hundred when we sample batches containing 10 per cent defectives the sample plan will signal us to screen. We have stipulated nothing about batches between or outside 5 and 10 per cent defective; we know, however, that if we can expect the plan to tell us to accept 5 per cent defective batches 80 per cent of the time, then it will tell us to accept less-than-5 per cent defective batches more than 80 per cent of the time, and as long as it tells us to screen 10 per cent defective batches 75 per cent of the time, it will tell us to screen more-than-10 per cent defective batches more than 75 per cent of the time. Between 5 and 10 per cent defectives, the plan will tell us to accept the batches close to 5 per cent less than 80 per cent of the time and to screen the batches close to 10 per cent less than 75 per cent of the time.

Once we have chosen the 5 and 10 per cent defective percentages and the 80 and 75 per cent probabilities, statistical theory will tell us the sampling plan to use. That is, the theory will tell how large the sample must be and how many defectives in a sample we are to take as the signal to screen.

Now we will look at the Bayesian method of finding a sampling plan. We said above that we would like to screen batches with large percentages of defectives and accept batches with small percentages of defectives. Implicit in this statement was a belief that it costs less to screen batches with large percentages of defectives than it does to accept them, and that it costs less to accept than to screen batches with low percentages of defectives. The Bayesian method requires that these costs be made explicit.

For a given percentage of defectives in a batch we determine the cost of screening and the cost of accepting. The cost of screening is simply the cost of examining every part in the batch and rejecting the defectives. The cost of accepting will be a little harder to determine. It is the cost of the delay, inconvenience, and any other undesirable results of leaving the defectives in the production process until they are found there. We now know for this percentage of defectives in a batch not only whether we would rather screen or accept the batch, but exactly how many dollars difference it makes. This is being explicit about what was implicit in our decision above to be satisfied if we screened batches that were 10 per cent defective, that is, "very bad" batches, 80 per cent of the time. If we knew exactly how many defectives were in each batch, our work would be over. But we do not know, and we must calculate the cost of screening and the cost of accepting for every possible percentage of defectives. The cost of screening is probably independent of the percentage of defectives; it will depend only on the size of the batch. But the cost of accepting will rise as the percentage of defectives rises.

Once we know the cost of screening and the cost of accepting for each possible percentage of defectives, we begin to examine sampling plans. For any given sampling plan we want to know the probability that it will tell us to screen, and the probability that it will tell us to accept, a batch with any given percentage of defectives. What we are doing is similar to one of the steps in the classical method, where we were looking for a plan that would offer us a probability of 80 per cent of telling us to accept a batch that was 5 per cent defective.

Now, for a given sampling plan and for each possible percentage of defectives in a batch we have the cost of screening the batch, the cost of accepting it, the probability that our sampling plan will tell us to screen the batch, and the probability that our plan will tell us to accept it. In each case, we multiply the cost of screening by the probability of the plan telling us to screen and we multiply the cost of accepting by the probability of the plan telling us to accept, and add the results. This is the "expected cost" of using the given sampling plan for each percentage of defectives. The expected cost is a sort of combination of measurable costs and the probabilities that these costs will actually be incurred.

Now, for the given sampling plan and for each possible percentage of defectives in a batch we have an expected cost associated with that plan. Our next step is to use our experience to establish the probability that a batch will have each of these possible percentages of defectives. This is the point where the Bayesian approach differs radically from the classical approach. Nowhere in the classical method did we consider the probability of a batch containing any particular percentage of defectives. But now we multiply for each possible percentage of defectives, the probability that a batch will contain that percentage of defectives by the expected cost associated with the sampling plan. We add all these to arrive at the expected cost for the whole range of percentages of defectives. If we add in the cost of performing the sampling itself, we will have the expected cost for the sampling plan—a single dollar figure associated with that plan.

Now we repeat the process for all sampling plans. (Statistical theory and mathematical methods help to keep this operation less tedious than it might seem from the foregoing discussion.) We then have an expected cost associated with each sampling plan, and we simply choose the sampling plan that offers the lowest expected cost. That is, we choose the plan that we expect will result in the lowest overall cost, counting costs of sampling, costs of screening, and costs of accepting.

The Bayesian method probably seems much more difficult to use than the classical method. But recall that the classical method required establishing numerical criteria with no precise basis for doing this. The Bayesian method requires explicit handling of costs. And the classical method incorporates none of the benefit of the best estimate we could make of the probability of a batch containing any particular percentage of defectives, an estimate that might be quite reliable if we have some experience with the parts.

References

In this chapter we have tried to provide a brief introduction to statistics in business research without venturing into a technical and mathematical discussion. To progress much farther the reader will have to become familiar with some of the mathematics involved, and for those who wish to read more on the subject we suggest the following books:

JOHN E. FREUND AND FRANK J. WILLIAMS, *Elementary Business Statistics,* Englewood Cliffs, N.J.: Prentice-Hall, Inc., 1964.
This is an introductory textbook on business statistics.

M. J. MORONEY, *Facts from Figures,* Baltimore: Penguin Books, Inc., 3d and rev. ed., 1957.
This inexpensive book deals in a very simple way with statistics and their uses. The discussion is not primarily in terms of business use of statistics, but many business applications are described.

ROBERT SCHLAIFER, *Introduction to Statistics for Business Decisions,* New York: McGraw-Hill Book Company, 1961.
This is an introductory textbook dealing with Bayesian statistics and their use in business.

ROBERT SCHLAIFER, *Probability and Statistics for Business Decisions,* New York: McGraw-Hill Book Company, 1959.
This is a more difficult book than the preceding and covers a wider range of topics.

W. A. WALLIS AND H. V. ROBERTS, *Statistics: A New Approach,* New York: The Free Press of Glencoe, 1956.
This is a simple statistics textbook, written for students with no previous experience in statistics, and useful for business applications.

7
ORGANIZATION OF A REPORT

Once you have clearly established in your own mind the purpose of your report, completed your research, and reached your conclusions, you face the job of working out the presentation of your material. The most important aspect of this presentation is organization.

Most businessmen are literate enough to avoid obvious mistakes in spelling and grammar. Generally, their choice of words is not bad. But relatively few businessmen are able to do a good job on the overall organization of a report. Yet the absence of such organization is detected by almost any reader, although he may not be aware of precisely what is wrong. When a businessman complains that the reports he is given are badly written, but cannot explain exactly what is wrong, the chances are that they are poorly organized.

Organize to Suit Your Reader's Needs

Working out the overall organization of a report is difficult. As we demonstrated in Chapter 1, it goes hand in hand with establishing precisely what the purposes of the report are to be.

Suppose you have been asked by your office manager to investigate and report to him how companies handle the mail they receive. The office manager wants to know whether your company can eliminate the expense, in large mailings, of typing the recipients' addresses on letters. The addresses are on the envelopes, of course. The principal purpose of your report seems fairly clear: You know a decision must be made, and so you collect the data necessary to make it. When you come to the writing of the report, however, you have to think through its purposes in more detail.

Let us look at one way in which you might organize your report:

Statement of the Problem
Method of Getting the Information
    1. You have sent out a questionnaire to 1,000 companies
    2. Here is how they were selected
    3. Here is the questionnaire sent
Results of the Study
    1. You have received replies from 490 companies, divided by size as follows:
        a. 79 replies from companies with fewer than 50 employees
        b. 153 from companies with 50 to 500 employees

    c. 81 from companies with more than 500 employees

    d. 177 from companies among the 1,000 largest in the United States

Conclusions

Since the study shows:

1. A majority in all categories, except companies with fewer than 50 employees, pass mail on to individuals with the envelope unopened.
2. Even when the envelope is opened in the mail room or by other employees, the envelope is attached to the contents.
3. Of all firms answering, 87 per cent—and, significantly, 95 per cent of the largest companies, where mail could be misdirected more easily—either pass the mail on unopened or attach the envelopes to the contents.

You can, therefore, conclude that:

1. Your company need not go to the extra expense of double-addressing direct mail.
2. However, it will have an added obligation to have the outside envelope in the most presentable form, since the great percentage of recipients actually see it.

Notice the implicit assumptions here as to purpose. You are assuming the office manager wants a recommendation, not merely information. You are assuming he wants a systematic, fairly detailed presentation. If he wants only conclusions, he will find this report tedious reading. If he wants conclusions first, reasoning second, and the details behind the reasoning last, so he can read first what he needs to know and then go on as far as he likes for supporting reasoning, you probably have organized your report backwards.

You are assuming, too, that the manager will want to read the questionnaire and list of companies. If he doesn't, then this information should be attached as an exhibit which is clearly optional or supplementary reading, and not put before the reader so he has to wade through it, or thinks he has to.

All these assumptions should have been carefully thought through before the outline was prepared. At the least, you should review them carefully before you proceed to write the report.

Organize for Clarity

In Chapter 2 we talked about organization to achieve clarity and coherence. This is especially important in a report, which may be long and complicated. You must give your reader conclusions, observations, and analysis at the right time. Remember that he never knows what is coming on the next page and that his memory is not perfect. Avoid statements that are meaningful to a reader only if he recalls all the details he has read or that become meaningful only after he reads on much further.

Here is an example. The writer of the report from which the following passage is taken was asked to appraise the opportunities for, the limitations to, growth of a corporation called Kapok Ice Cream Stores. Kapok operates a chain of stores which sell ice cream and sandwiches, and the company manufactures its own ice cream and sandwich fillings. The management was trying to develop plans for expansion. As you read the following passage, keep in mind the purpose for which this report was supposed to have been written.

Kapok's present market area offers a good opportunity for growth. At present most of its stores are within a 50-mile radius of the company's manufacturing plant. There are several important communities within 50 miles of the plant which do not have Kapok shops. Practically all of Connecticut, Rhode Island, and Massachusetts (except Cape Cod) are within a 100-mile radius of Kapok's plant. Kapok should be able to open stores throughout these three states because there are many large communities which are rapidly growing and because there are good roads which will make delivery easy.

General conditions make the opportunity for growth good. Average personal income is increasing every year. The population of the three southern New England states is growing rapidly. The *Kiplinger Washington Letter* forecasts that, between 1960 and 1975, Connecticut's population will increase 45 per cent, Massachusetts' will increase 19 per cent, and Rhode Island's will increase 15 per cent. The increasing population means an increasing number of potential customers.

Many factors of Kapok's internal structure provide opportunity for growth. High quality and reasonable price of Kapok's ice cream should help new stores to be successful. Since it has a quality product and since it has been growing rapidly, Kapok must have a good reputation in its area. This reputation should provide a good opportunity for expansion. The two owners are largely responsible for the growing sales volume because they make all the decisions. These men should take advantage of their managerial abilities to expand the business. The management training program, which is a result of the owners' efforts, is providing an opportunity for expansion because of the many managers that it produces. Since the owners make all of the decisions, they are responsible for the company's good financial position.

For convenience, we call the preceding three paragraphs Part I of the report. Part II follows below. In the actual report, Part II followed with no indication of any break in the train of thought.

Two forms of competition are limitations to Kapok's growth. The first form is ice cream's related products. Since 1951, national per capita consumption of ice cream has remained nearly constant while per capita consumption of related products has increased 205 per cent. Kapok's production per store has remained relatively fixed during the same time period. If sales of related products continue to increase, as the trend indicates, Kapok's growth will be limited to the rate of population increase.

The other form of competition that may limit Kapok's growth is other shops which sell ice cream. The company's president feels that Kapok stores are seldom affected by competition. If the company expands, it probably will go into new areas. The owners may find that businesses serving and selling ice cream may compete with them in these new areas. If they find competitors, their growth may be limited.

Some parts of the company's present internal structure are limitations to growth. Today the size of the business permits the two owners to keep close control over the business because they are in close contact with it. If the number of stores and the size of the market area are increased under the present organization, the owners would lose their close contact with the stores. There is an apparent lack of planning by the owners. For instance, the president doesn't know where they will be opening seven new stores planned for 1960, which is only a year away. When the president doesn't know where the new stores will be in a year, it is no surprise when he states that growth has continually been underestimated.

The writer here has set out to appraise opportunities for, and limitations to, growth of the Kapok company. He has taken this assignment quite literally, and has decided to present first the opportunities and, second, the limitations. This may have seemed to him a very sensible plan of organization, and it may seem that way to you until you think about it a little and until you read through these two parts carefully. Part I presents the reader with an extremely optimistic statement of opportunity. We can summarize this optimism in the form of three general conclusions the writer has reached:

1. The growth potential of the Kapok company is not limited geographically because there are vast areas into which the company has not yet penetrated.
2. There will be a boom in the demand for ice cream because personal income and population are increasing.
3. The owners of the company, who are extremely competent, are solely responsible for the company's past successes because they make all the decisions.

At the end of Part I, a reader is going to be quite optimistic about the success of the company. He has been led to believe there are virtually no obstacles to continued growth. He certainly is not expecting a pessimistic final conclusion. The reader is in for disillusionment. The conclusions reached by the writer in Part II might be summarized as follows:

1. The growth potential of the company *is* limited geographically because Kopak will encounter competition in its attempt to penetrate new areas.
2. There will *not* be a boom in the demand for ice cream because products related to ice cream are capturing an increasing share of the market.
3. Expansion will force the company's owners to *relinquish* much of their control over company policy. Furthermore, the owners are pretty poor planners.

What Part II seems to do, then, is virtually contradict the specific points justifying the optimism in Part I. The reader is likely to be disappointed, confused, and perhaps angry. The writer has not played fair with him. It is all very well in a mystery story to lead the reader to think the butler is the murderer and then on the last page to reveal it was the housemaid after all, but the writer of a business report plays games like this with his reader at his own peril.

We have said that Part II seems to contradict Part I. And yet this is really just an appearance. The writer could have said just about what he has said in Parts I and II, avoiding the appearance of contradiction and presenting a fairly balanced view of the limitations and opportunities. To begin with, he could have put all his conclusions together. He could have considered both geographical limitations and opportunities in one place, instead of telling the reader about the geographical opportunities for growth on one page and discussing the limitations long afterward. He could also have used transitional words like *nevertheless* to link the pros and cons and to lead to a conclusion reflecting a balance of the two.

There are other ways in which the writer could have organized his report to avoid the appearance of inconsistency and to avoid misleading his reader. He could have warned the reader, for example, that he would first discuss opportunities, then limitations, and perhaps finally present a summary which would pull the two together and lead to a recommendation.

Here is how another person handled precisely the same assignment. There are obvious writing defects in the following three paragraphs, but notice how the overall organization has overcome the faults of the preceding report.

Upon examination of a map of New England, I found that there are several heavily populated areas that have not been exploited by Kapok. Such areas include Boston, Providence, the north shore area adjacent to Boston, and Cape Cod. These last are particularly attractive because of their popularity as summer resort areas. It is true that Howard Johnson is firmly entrenched in the Boston area. However, as a restaurant, the appeal of Howard Johnson is differentiated from the appeal of Kapok as an ice cream specialty shop. Thus, in the near future, Kapok's expansion should not be limited by geography.

While the per capita consumption of ice cream in the United States appears to be leveling off or declining slightly, the rising population still indicates expanding consumption. In addition,

Kapok's growth indicates an increasing share of the market, so that the rate of per capita consumption should not serve as a deterrent to future growth.

However, growth will require that the corporation become more decentralized. The owners will not be able to devote time to every operating decision. Just how much their personalities have stimulated the growth of the corporation in the past is a matter of conjecture. However, their unique achievement would indicate that they are highly talented individuals and that their personal contribution must have been substantial. If the growth pattern of Kapok is to be maintained, managerial talent of this same high caliber must be developed.

Notice what the second writer has done in contrast to what the first writer did. He has discussed one by one the topics that he thinks relate to limitations and opportunity, and he has drawn a conclusion for each topic. For example, he discusses the geographical topic in one place, pointing out its opportunities and its limitations and finishing with what he thinks is a fair overall evaluation of the importance of geographical factors to the company. The second writer does not mislead or disillusion his reader. The reader at no point is led to expect a conclusion different from the one given to him.

Notice another significant distinction between what the first and what the second writer has done. The first presentation is rather like a debate. The affirmative has its innings first, and then the negative presents its case. It is left to the reader to put the two arguments together and form a conclusion. The second writer puts the arguments together himself. One way of describing this distinction is to say that the first writer has simply provided the facts, while the second writer has given the facts and used them to come to a conclusion. Which method is correct for any particular report, of course, depends on the purpose of the report. Is it simply to furnish facts, or is it to give conclusions or helpful advice? The assignment for this report seemed to require the latter.

On the basis of the examples we have looked at, you should be getting some idea of what is involved in the overall organization of a report. Here are some of the questions you may have to answer when you begin to design a report:

1. Should I state my conclusion at the beginning and then show what led me to that conclusion, or should I state the problem at the beginning, follow this with a logical analysis, and end up with a conclusion?
2. If I have been asked to write a report selecting one of several alternatives on the basis of the application of several criteria, should I discuss the alternatives one at a time, applying all the criteria to each alternative, or should I deal with the criteria one at a time, applying each criterion to all the alternatives?

Questions like these are sometimes very difficult to answer. In some situations it may seem almost impossible to come up with an overall organization that is clearly the best one and thus makes it easy for your reader to follow exactly what you are saying. But at least keep your reader clearly in mind. You are writing the report for him, and it is his convenience you are trying to serve. In general, you are trying to present a coherent whole. You want him to progress through your report without confusion, without surprises, without wondering what you are talking about or where you have gotten your information and conclusions. You want him to understand, all the way through, what it is you are trying to tell him. You do not want him to feel he was misled. You do not want to lead him to believe that you will reach one conclusion and then suddenly reach another. It should be obvious to your reader why every statement in your report is there and why it is where you have put it.

8

PUTTING A REPORT TOGETHER

In the preceding chapter, we discussed in some detail the organization of a report, and we evaluated the organization of actual reports. In this chapter, we will formulate the outline for a management consultant's report, beginning with his findings, and discuss some of the techniques of writing it up. We begin with a statement of the problem and of the purpose of the report.

In the late 1950's the management of a company manufacturing bicycles in the United States became concerned about a decline in sales and almost vanishing profits. The company faced intense competition from other United States manufacturers, and even more serious competition from foreign manufacturers, whose production costs were much lower than those of any United States company. The foreign companies were able to undersell any American manufacturer by a wide margin, and although they had captured less than half of the domestic market, their share was rising steadily. The company asked a management consultant for his recommendations.

After analyzing the problems of the company, the consultant reached a number of conclusions. The following paragraphs summarize these conclusions in outline form. The problem is to organize them into a logical presentation.

1. The company could reduce its costs by importing parts from Europe instead of buying them from United States parts manufacturers. European parts are much cheaper and are of equal quality.
2. The tariff on imported bicycles is now 11.25 per cent on lightweight bicycles and 22.5 per cent on all others. These rates were raised, in 1955, from 7.5 per cent and 15 per cent, after an urgent appeal by the domestic manufacturers. The lower rates had been instituted in 1948, when, under the General Agreement on Tariffs and Trade, the normal rate of 30 per cent was reduced. The company could join with others in the industry to urge the restoration of the original 30 per cent duty, but it would not be practical to attempt to persuade Congress to raise the rate beyond that. Although even a 30 per per cent duty would still permit foreign manufacturers to undersell United States manufacturers, the higher rate would help the domestic companies. In fact it would be more effective than would importing the parts.

   To obtain a higher rate, however, it would be important for the entire domestic industry, both bicycle manufacturers and parts manufacturers, to present a united front. The parts manufacturers might be unwilling to support a plea for higher tariffs on bicycles if the domestic bicycle manufacturers imported parts.

3. Foreign bicycle manufacturers are taking a larger share of the United States market every year. Even if the company were to buy its parts in Europe *and* have the tariff restored to 30 per cent, it still could not meet the prices of foreign-made bicycles. There is no significant appeal that can be made to buyers of bicycles that will offset the effect of the lower price of the foreign bicycles.

4. An increase in the tariff on bicycles to 30 per cent would be of some help, but a quota on imports would be even more helpful. True, foreign manufacturers could still undersell domestic manufacturers, but there would be a limit to the number of bicycles that could be imported. The growth of the foreign companies' share of the market would thus be halted. A united industry might be able to persuade the President to impose such quotas. As in the case of an appeal for higher tariffs, it would be important to have the support of the parts manufacturers.

5. The company should diversify its manufacturing activities by making products other than bicycles. Bicycle manufacturing in the United States has no future. Even if quotas were to prevent foreign manufacturers from obtaining a larger share of the market, the company would still be unable to make a reasonable profit on its bicycles.

6. The middleweight bicycle, introduced only two years ago, seems to offer the best opportunity for the company, at least in the short run. Foreign manufacturers have captured a large part of the market for lightweight and regular-weight bicycles, but have not entered the middleweight market.

7. If the company imports parts, the American parts manufacturers may cease making important parts. This would leave the company, and other domestic bicycle manufacturers, with no local source of supply.

8. If the company decides to continue the manufacture of bicycles, it should import some parts. Any risk involved is more than offset by the cost savings. Other United States manufacturers are already importing parts.

9. The company should try to persuade the industry to press for import quotas. If quotas are not obtainable, the next best thing is higher tariffs.

10. If a quota or higher tariffs were obtained, foreign bicycle manufacturers might retaliate by bringing pressure on foreign parts manufacturers to stop them from selling parts to the American manufacturers.

The report assignment clearly asked for recommendations, so these must be stated somewhere. It is hard to know exactly how much reasoning and analysis will be expected in support of the recommendations, but we do know that the recommendations include at least one that may seem rather startling and may be quite unwelcome —the recommendation to diversify because there is no future in the bicycle industry. This recommendation will require considerable support. We will assume that the 10 groups of statements contain all the reasoning that the consultant can offer, and that any detailed data to support this reasoning will be presented in exhibits or an appendix.

The first thing we have to do is to sort these 10 groups of statements into a reasonable selection of topics. For convenience, we will refer to the groups of statements by their numbers.

Group 1 sets forth the advantages of importing bicycle parts. We can begin, then, by selecting as one topic the importation of parts and identifying the other groups of statements that relate to this topic. Groups 2 and 4 deal with its relation to tariffs and quotas; 3 evaluates the effectiveness of importing parts; 7 and 10 point out the risks and dangers involved; and 8 is a conclusion about whether or not to import parts.

The second major topic is the possibility of obtaining an increase in the tariff. This topic is introduced and discussed in 2; a conclusion as to the effectiveness of an increase in tariffs is drawn in 3; in 4 and 9 quotas are compared with higher tariffs and a conclusion is drawn as to which would be better; and 10 sets forth the warning that higher tariffs might endanger the availability of foreign parts.

In 3, we find a third topic: the inability of the company to meet foreign prices no matter what it does. Group 5 contains the recommendation that the company diversify because there is no future in bicycle manufacturing. Groups 3 and 5, combined, draw an overall conclusion and constitute what is probably the most important topic.

The possibility of obtaining a quota forms a fourth topic. This topic is discussed in group 4, and is compared there to tariff increases and related to the topic of importing parts. A conclusion as to what should be done about quotas is drawn in 9, and 10 again relates quotas to the importation of parts.

Finally, a fifth topic, production of middleweight bicycles, is discussed in 6.

We now have a set of five major topics out of which we can build a report. You may not entirely agree with this set of topics. For example, it may seem to you that tariffs and quotas are really one topic, not two. In most reports there is no single "right" selection of topics. You have to make what you think will appear to your reader to be a reasonable selection. We will assume that these five topics constitute a reasonable selection, and proceed to the next stage.

Our next job is to organize the topics into a logical sequence. One step in this process seems fairly obvious. There is a clear distinction between the third topic—the overall conclusion that there is no future in the manufacturing of bicycles and that the company ought to diversify—and the other four topics, all of which deal with ways in which the company might be more successful at bicycle manufacturing. We can now see the report as consisting of two parts. One will be the recommendation that the company diversify, and not pin its hopes on manufacturing bicycles. The other will be a set of recommendations for the company to follow so long as it continues to manufacture bicycles. We certainly will not place the overall conclusion, topic 3, in the midst of the other topics. Having found a clear and logical division of the report into two parts, we are not going to sacrifice clarity and logic by mixing the two parts up. And there is another reason. The two positions of importance in a report are the beginning and the end. A reader will probably look closely at these two parts of the report, no matter how quickly he scans the remainder, and he will expect to find anything of importance in one of these two positions. Our basic conclusion, topic 3, is much too important to be buried somewhere near the center of the report. It must come at the beginning or the end. Which will it be?

One factor to consider is that the discussion of what the company should do as long as it continues to manufacture bicycles contains the justification for the conclusion that there is no future in this manufacture. It is this discussion which points out that even the importation of parts and the raising of the tariff will not enable the company to meet the prices of foreign competitors. If we put the general conclusion last, it would follow logically from the discussion of whether bicycles can profitably be manufactured. There is one objection to this sequence. The first part of the report may seem to imply that the company should continue to make bicycles, and when the reader comes to the final conclusion he may feel unfairly let down. Perhaps it would be better to warn him in the beginning that our conclusion is that bicycle manufacturing has no future. But we may also be concerned over the reader's reaction to our conclusion. If it is going to come as a shock to the company's management, then perhaps we would do better to lead up to it gradually. We could put the overall conclusion at the end of the report, building up enough pessimism in the first part so that the reader will not be surprised at our conclusion.

The question of sequence here is not an easy one to answer. We will make the assumption that the management of the company will not be shocked by our conclusion into dropping the report and reading no further. We will begin by stating our basic conclusion. But we will point out quickly that if the management does not wish to act on this recommendation, or if they intend to continue bicycle manufacturing for at least a while, we have a set of recommendations to assist them. This will ensure that our overall conclusion reaches the reader quickly. At the same time, it will provide a convenient introduction to the second part of our report, which will deal with the remaining four topics.

Our organization now is:

I. Basic conclusion: Diversify.
II. Things to do if manufacturing continues: tariffs, quotas, parts importation, and middleweight bicycles.

Our problem now is to organize the four topics in Part II: tariffs, quotas, importation of parts, and middleweight bicycles. We can draw at least two conclusions fairly quickly. One is that the topic of middleweight bicycles does not seem to have a logical connection with the others. For the moment, then, let us set this topic aside. Our other conclusion is that tariffs and quotas seem to be closely related. We can assume that these two will be discussed in conjunction with each other: We will discuss either tariffs and then quotas or quotas and then tariffs.

As we plan the sequence of topics, one thing must be kept in mind. We have to have transitions between topics. That is, there must be a logical basis for switching the topic under discussion from, say, parts to tariffs, or from tariffs to quotas. Sometimes these transitions are hard to find. We want to make the best use of the transitions we have. We can anticipate trouble with the topic of middleweight bicycles, for example, but we should have no trouble providing a transition from tariffs to quotas or vice versa. We have a conclusion, in 9, that higher tariffs are desirable but that quotas would be even better, and this should provide the logical connection between the two topics.

We also have two good transitions between the topic of importation of parts and the topics of tariffs and quotas. The importation of parts might jeopardize success in obtaining higher tariffs or quotas, because the parts manufacturers might not join the bicycle manufacturers in requesting them. And one disadvantage of higher tariffs or quotas is that foreign manufacturers might retaliate by applying pressure to cut off the supply of foreign parts, a supply that would be crucial if domestic manufacturers were to stop making important parts.

We might begin by deciding whether to discuss tariffs before quotas or quotas before tariffs. The transition between the two topics will be based on the conclusion that quotas are preferable to tariffs. It probably does not make much difference whether we discuss quotas, reach the conclusion that they are desirable, point out that a less attractive substitute would be a higher tariff, and then proceed to discuss how to obtain a higher tariff; or whether we first discuss tariffs, reach the conclusion that a tariff increase would be desirable, point out that a quota would be even better, and then go on to discuss quotas. However, since our conclusion is that quotas are better, it may seem more logical to start with tariffs and then discuss quotas and conclude that quotas are better rather than to start with quotas, then discuss tariffs, and then backtrack to the conclusion that quotas are better. Our decision, then, is to discuss tariffs, then quotas.

   I. Basic conclusion: Diversify.
  II. Things to do if manufacturing continues:
     A. Seek higher tariffs.
     B. Seek quotas.

Our next question is whether to discuss parts before tariffs or after quotas. We could begin with parts, discuss the advantages and disadvantages of importing them, and draw the conclusion that the saving in cost is worth the risk involved. We could then point out that importing parts might jeopardize the company's success in obtaining a higher tariff or a quota, and proceed to discuss tariffs. One difficulty in this arrangement is that it is not quite logical to draw the conclusion that the saving is worth the risk before we even refer to the risk that the importation of parts might jeopardize the effort to obtain quotas or higher tariffs. We would like to draw our final conclusion about importing parts after we have discussed *all* the advantages and disadvantages.

Let's consider discussing tariffs and quotas first, and then moving to parts. We could discuss the advantages and limitations of a higher tariff, point out that a quota would be even better, and draw the conclusion that the company should press for a quota. We could then discuss the need for a united industry in obtaining a quota and the danger of alienating the parts manufacturers by importing. We could then go on to a discussion of importing parts. But we still have to work in the point that one disadvantage of higher tariffs and quotas is that foreign bicycle manufacturers might retaliate by closing off foreign supplies of parts. We could use this as part of our transition from quotas to parts, but again we are drawing a conclusion—that the company should seek a quota—and later bringing up a new disadvantage. We have the same logical difficulty we ran into when we put the parts discussion first.

We may decide at this point that we will first have to discuss all three topics—importing parts, appealing for a higher tariff, and seeking a quota—before drawing any conclusions at all. Our organization might then be: parts, tariffs, quotas, conclusion; or tariffs, quotas, parts, conclusion. A choice between these alternatives may not be the only method of handling the topics, but since it appears to resolve the dilemma described in the preceding two paragraphs, it is the method we will use.

Before choosing between the two sequences, we should consider one further factor. Both transitions, between parts and tariffs or between quotas and parts, require bringing in a disadvantage: in the one case, that involved in importing parts; in the other, that involved in quotas or higher tariffs. So long as we are going to recommend the importation of parts, we may prefer not to introduce the topic with a disadvantage; but the same consideration applies to tariffs and quotas. The reasoning here is that a pessimistic introduction to a topic makes it harder to reach an optimistic conclusion in a logical way. It would be better to start with the advantages, build up a strong case, and then concede a disadvantage as we move to the next topic. You may not agree with this. Actually, it is sometimes very effective to begin with the disadvantages and move to the advantages before drawing a positive conclusion. But this procedure usually works best where the disadvantages can be refuted or where the advantages nicely balance the disadvantages, canceling them out. The writer is really setting up apparent disadvantages and then knocking them down. But we have no answer to the disadvantages we raise, except to say that they don't outweigh the advantages; therefore we will try to avoid introducing our topics with disadvantages.

We could arrange the topics this way: (1) parts, disadvantageous effect of importing parts on tariffs and quotas; (2) tariffs, preference for quotas; (3) quotas, disadvantageous effect of tariffs and quotas on importation of parts; (4) conclusion. Or we could use this arrangement: (1) tariffs, preference for quotas; (2) quotas, disadvantageous effect of tariffs and quotas on importation of parts; (3) parts, disadvantageous effect of importing parts on tariffs and quotas; (4) conclusion. It probably doesn't make any difference which of these sequences we choose. We will use the first.

This still leaves the topic of middleweight bicycles. It will have to come either before the discussion of parts or after our conclusion relating to parts, tariffs, and quotas. It can be connected with any of these topics only through the fact that it offers another way to improve sales and profits. Let's consider putting it last. If we put it at the end of the report, it may seem to dangle almost as an afterthought, because of the weak logical transition. The end position, too, is one of importance, and the middleweight topic does not seem any more important than any of the others. Our conclusion to the parts–tariffs–quotas discussion seems to be quite important, if only because it pulls together three topics. It seems best, therefore, to place this conclusion at the end and put the middleweight bicycle topic before the parts topic.

Our final organization (transitions are shown in parentheses) is as follows:

I. Basic conclusion: Diversify; there is no future in bicycle manufacturing. . . . (But so long as bicycle manufacturing continues, there are—)

II. Things to do if manufacturing continues:

    A. Emphasize manufacture of middleweight bicycles. . . . (Another step to consider is—)

    B. Importation of parts. . . . (A disadvantage of this is that it may jeopardize success in obtaining—)

    C. Higher tariffs. . . . (These would not be as effective, however, as—)

    D. Quotas. . . . (Although both higher tariffs and quotas might jeopardize the supply of parts, we can come to a positive—)

    E. Conclusion: The company should import parts, press for quotas or tariffs, and emphasize production of middleweight bicycles.

9
BEGINNINGS AND ENDINGS

The two most important parts of any business report are its beginning and its ending. You can generally count on both of these being read. Often, if the reader is in a hurry or not particularly interested, these are the only parts that are read. But, of course, a well-designed beginning or ending may persuade an otherwise hurried or uninterested businessman to read a report through.

Beginnings

Most people, until they have had a lot of practice writing on a wide variety of topics, find the composing of the first sentence of a letter or report a painful process. Many letter writers give up and reach for the telephone. But if the telephone will not do, as is usually the case when a report is called for, you must somehow overcome this initial hurdle and get on with the job. There are several approaches that may be helpful.

Many writers recommend that if you cannot think of the right beginning for your first draft, you skip it and go on to something else. Start with some specific description or analysis. You will probably think of an appropriate beginning later—perhaps by the time you have writen a paragraph or two, perhaps not until you have finished the whole report. It is usually much better to write up the material you feel able to handle and set the harder parts aside. It is easier to fill in the gaps than to struggle to produce a perfect document the first time through.

If you don't like leaving gaps, then simply write any sort of beginning, no matter how poor, and get on with the rest of the writing. You can then come back and think of a better beginning later. As a matter of fact, you are quite likely to find that you come up with an excellent beginning in the second, third, or fourth paragraph, or even later, and that all you have to do is transpose the material or discard your first paragraph or two.

Another way to get started is to imagine that the person you are writing to is sitting across your desk. How would you begin a conversation about your topic? Use this as the beginning of your report.

All this means that it is simply not worth waiting for the perfect beginning to leap into your mind. Sooner or later, of course, you will have to write a good beginning.

Elements of a beginning

There are at least three elements that may be called for in a beginning. One is a simple statement of what the communication is all about. For example, you might begin a letter by saying: "You have requested a list of the distributors of our product in eastern New Jersey. The list follows." Or you might start a report by saying: "This report analyzes the profitability of our product X and deals with the question of whether we should reduce its price." This kind of statement tells the reader what he is going to read about. It is useful to the writer, too. He can check back on it once in a while to see if he is really talking about what he promised to discuss.

The second element is a statement of the writer's proposition, thesis, or conclusion. For example, your letter might begin: "Our distributor located nearest to your business is the X Company. I am sure you will find the people there helpful and courteous." Or your report might begin: "Our product X is currently not as profitable as it could be, and its price should be lowered 50 cents per unit." This kind of statement tells the reader right away what the point of your communication is. Again, it serves as a useful guide to the writer, who can ask himself, as he goes on with his writing, whether he is sticking to the point.

The third element is a statement to catch the reader's interest, to persuade him that what you have to say is important and that he should take the trouble to read it. For example, your letter might begin: "You will find that our distributors can help you to make money." Or your report might begin: "Our product X is currently unprofitable, and unless we reduce its price it can lead the company into serious trouble."

Any particular piece of writing may require, in its beginning, one, two, or all three of these elements. It may require none of them, although this is unlikely. Sometimes you may feel that your reader already knows what your report is about, especially if he asked for it, and that there is no need to tell him in your introduction. But before you come to this conclusion, there are a few possibilities you should consider. It may well be that by the time he receives your report, he will have forgotten his request. Or he may have forgotten exactly what he requested. This is especially possible if the request was made much earlier or if he has requested many reports. In many cases, even when the reader remembers exactly what it was he asked for, he may be interested in knowing whether you understood him. He may expect to find, at the beginning of your communication, an assurance that you are going to give him exactly what he asked for. If there is any doubt in your mind whether your reader needs or wants this information, you had better put it in.

There is an important advantage in this first element of a beginning. It is usually very easy to write. All you have to do is decide what the content of your letter or report is, and then describe it in a sentence. We will soon discuss some reasons why this may not be the most effective first sentence of a report, but if you cannot think of any other way to start off, you can always fall back on a simple statement of what the report is all about.

Here is an opening paragraph restricted entirely to this first element. It is from a report replying to a request for an analysis and appraisal of a company's situation.

(1) As you have requested, I have analyzed the current situation of the company. My analysis will be presented in three sections: first a group of general comments, then a discussion of specific strengths and weaknesses in the company's position, and finally a conclusion based upon them.

The second element, a statement of the writer's recommendation or conclusion, is useful in that it gives the reader something to focus his attention on. It tells him why you have written the kind of report that you have. You may have written an analysis or appraisal in response to a request. But this, alone, does not explain the kind of analysis you have written. Once the reader knows what your recommendation is, he can relate everything you say to that recommendation, and what you say becomes that much more meaningful. At times, you may not want to state your recommendation at the beginning of your written communication. For one thing, you may be afraid that it will produce an unfavorable reaction. In such a situation, you may want to lead up to your conclusion gradually. Or you may simply feel you cannot express your recommendation or conclusion in one sentence, or even in one short paragraph. In this case, you are perhaps only wasting your reader's time if you try to describe your conclusion concisely. Here is an example from another report written in response to the same request.

> (2) We are faced with current liabilities of more than one million dollars and the necessity of meeting an annual sinking fund payment plus interest of about $100,000, while we possess only $800,000 in cash. For these reasons, this company must take immediate action to increase sales if it is to stay in business.

This beginning tells us immediately what the writer's conclusion is—immediate action to increase sales. He has not spelled out his recommendation—that is, he has not said how to increase sales—but he has shown us that increasing sales is his theme.

The third element, the statement designed to attract the reader's interest, is much less important in business communication than in almost any other kind of writing. Except in special situations—when you are writing sales literature, for example, or an article for a business journal—you can assume your reader's interest. The writer of an essay or a short story cannot make this assumption. He must awaken interest at the start and persuade the reader to go on. Still, if you are in any doubt whether the subject matter of your communication will seem important to your reader—and this is likely when you are writing on your own initiative and not in response to a request—it may be worthwhile to begin with a statement that will convince the reader of the importance of what he is going to read. Here is a third beginning for the report we have been discussing.

> (3) This company is in very serious trouble. The drain on cash caused by unanticipated capital expenditures, the drastic sales decline, and the consequent operating loss have put the company close to bankruptcy. Therefore, the most pressing problem is increasing sales to a profitable level.

Compare this with example (2). The first sentence, especially, is designed to catch the reader's attention and hold it. The writer of example (3) then goes on to state his theme or proposition. Observe, however, that the writer of example (2) has given us specific information. We can see more clearly what is wrong with the company from example (2). Although both include an indication of the writer's proposition as well as a statement designed to attract interest, the writer of (2) has stressed the former, while the writer of (3) has stressed the latter. Neither has shown any concern for the first element—describing what the report is all about—as the writer of example (1) did.

You may feel that example (1) is not so interesting or informative as it might be. You may also feel that examples (2) and (3) begin too abruptly and that there should be some introduction stating what the report is all about. Here is another example, offering within itself an interesting contrast between the two ways of beginning.

(4) The purpose of this report is to analyze this company's current position. On the basis of this analysis, the concluding section of the report will present the major issue to which the company must devote immediate attention.

The most striking characteristic of the company is a serious decline in sales which, unless corrected, could lead to bankruptcy in a short time. [The paragraph then went on to document this statement and draw a conclusion.]

The first paragraph of example (4) is very similar to example (1). The first sentence of the second paragraph is very similar to example (3), and somewhat similar to example (2). Some writers would simply strike out the first paragraph of example (4) and begin with the statement of the writer's proposition. A compromise between this and leaving example (4) as it stands might be to greatly abbreviate the first paragraph, leaving some explanation of what the report is all about, but moving very quickly to an attention-getting statement of the writer's proposition. Suppose we simply delete the second sentence of the first paragraph and move the first sentence of the second paragraph up:

The purpose of this report is to analyze the company's current position. The most striking characteristic of this position is a serious decline in sales which, unless corrected, could lead to bankruptcy in a short time.

Now we have a beginning that incorporates all three of the elements we have discussed.

We will now turn briefly to some nonbusiness writing for examples of different kinds of beginnings. Some of these are more interesting than the beginnings to business communications, and they provide more scope for exploring the writers' purposes and techniques.

Here is the beginning of a profile of Margaret Mead, published by *The New Yorker* magazine on December 30, 1961. The article is by Winthrop Sargeant and is titled "It's All Anthropology."

(5) In 1928, a precocious, attractive, rather fragile looking 26-year-old anthropologist named Margaret Mead published a book called *Coming of Age in Samoa,* which set several records for a work of its type. For one thing, it became a popular best seller.[1]

Of the three elements of a beginning that we have discussed, this example clearly emphasizes the third, attracting the reader's interest. And this is what we would expect of the beginning to a magazine article. There is some of the first element present, too. The writer is giving some indication of what his article is all about. And, of course, his title helped to explain his topic. There seems to be little or no trace of the second element, the statement of the writer's proposition or conclusion.

Here is a somewhat similar example, from an article by John Brooks in *The New Yorker* of May 26, 1962, titled "Annals of Business: The Impacted Philosophers."

(6) Among the greatest problems facing American industry today, one may learn by talking with any of a large number of industrialists who are not known to be especially given to pontificating, is "the problem of communication." This preoccupation with the difficulty of getting a thought out of one head and into another is something the industrialists share with a substantial number of intellectuals and creative writers, more and more of whom seem inclined to regard communication, or the lack of it, as one of the greatest problems not just of industry but of humanity.[2]

---

[1] Reprinted by permission of *The New Yorker.*
[2] Reprinted by permission of *The New Yorker.*

Again, the emphasis is clearly on the third element, attracting the reader's interest and indicating that the subject to be discussed is an important one. Again, there is no indication of the writer's conclusion or of his thesis. But his general topic seems quite clear.

Both these examples were designed to serve specific purposes in magazine articles, and both serve these purposes well. We can probably conclude that neither, certainly not the first, would be appropriate as the beginning of a business report, not because they are "bad" beginnings, but because a different set of purposes calls for a different sort of beginning.

To complete our survey, we will look at two examples of writing where the second element, the writer's proposition or conclusion, is stated rather forcefully. Here is an example from an article entitled "The Doctor's Lobby," by James Howard Means, M.D., that appeared in *The Atlantic Monthly* in October, 1950.

(7) Medical science has made enormous strides. Are the American people getting the greatest possible benefit from them? Obviously not! The majority cannot afford medical care under the prevailing fee-for-service system, and in many places adequate personnel and facilities are not available.[3]

This is clearly the beginning of an article by a writer who is on a crusade. He wastes no time telling us what his subject is, and he goes into no explanation as to why it is important. He simply states his proposition emphatically, and counts on this to arouse the reader's interest.

Contrast this beginning with the following one from an article titled "Everybody on Relief?" by Agnes E. Meyer. The article appeared in *The Atlantic Monthly* of January, 1950, and the author's proposition was that our system of social security is a bad one.

(8) A sound and comprehensive system of social insurance—in other words, earned security—is an intrinsic part of a positive approach to the nation's welfare. Nobody can deny that a broad and just distribution of social insurance is necessary today as a bulwark against the unavoidable hazards of modern industrial

[3] Reprinted by permission of *The Atlantic Monthly*.

society. Rightly used, social insurance can act as a fly wheel for the nation's economic and social stability.[4]

Notice that this beginning does not convey any indication of the writer's recommendation or conclusion. Nor does it convey any precise idea of just what the article is about. Whether it excites the reader's interest and makes him want to read on, you can judge for yourself. But your conclusion is likely to be that if this writer is on a crusade, as she actually was, she is taking a long time getting around to it.

After investigating different methods of beginning a communication, we are led back to our original theme—that *purpose* is all-important and that you must put yourself in your reader's place and ask yourself, "What would I want or need in an introduction to this report?" We have suggested some wants and needs, and some purposes, that are likely to be applicable. But only by thinking through the particular report you are about to write can you arrive at an appropriate beginning.

Endings

Concluding paragraphs are generally easier to write than beginning paragraphs. When you reach your concluding paragraph, you know what your report is all about; you know what conclusions you have reached, which are important and which less important; you know which will be most useful to the reader and which less useful; which he will probably be pleased to read about and which he may not like so much. You are in a position to sum up what you have to say. But, although one is easier to write than the other, the fact remains that the opening and the concluding paragraphs are the two most important paragraphs in any report. It is here you want to put what should be emphasized most.

One function of the concluding paragraph is to give the reader a sense of completeness. You want to let him know that you have said all you need to say, and he must be satisfied that your report is complete. Consider the following example. It is the last paragraph of a report written in response to a request for an analysis and

---

[4] Reprinted by permission of *The Atlantic Monthly*.

appraisal of a company's situation, with a recommendation for action.

(9) The President of the Company is in a state of poor health and there is some question as to the length of time that he will be able to remain as an active manager of the company. In early 1963, he was forced to retire from the active role of President for several months for reasons of poor health.

This paragraph gives the impression that the writer simply ran out of time, paper, or perhaps words, if he felt he had a word limit. We expect something more: some explanation of the importance of his conclusion and some recommendation for action. Here is a similar example:

(10) The credit terms given by this company may be too tight, since there have been no major bad debt losses for a long time. Tight credit, when the industry trend is toward very liberal credit, could harm sales, as could a shortening of the discount period.

Again, we are led to expect that a topic will be discussed more fully, but the writer simply stops. Contrast examples (9) and (10) with the following:

(11) I feel that this plan will enable your company to grow at a satisfactory rate. You may someday take your place as a national distributor, but you must grow into this stage gradually. I hope I have been of help in establishing the direction that you and your company should take in the future.

A second function of the concluding paragraph is to emphasize the things that you want to emphasize. You want to focus your reader's attention on the important matters and leave him with the proper perspective. Here is an example, again from a reply to a request for analysis and appraisal and recommendations for action.

(12) The President's selection of executives is further questioned, since he obviously has no one on his staff who can initiate ideas for new products, increased sales, or decreased costs. A vice-

president maintains strict credit policies, whereas a more lenient policy might result in more dealers and increased sales.

This conclusion rounds out the report somewhat better than examples (9) and (10), although the second sentence seems to start a new train of thought. But example (12) does not provide any emphasis. It does not single out any particular problem or course of action with which the reader should be left.

Here is another example, one that appears to be better:

(13) The Company's basic difficulties lie in a lack of planning and a superficial analysis of their management, marketing, and production problems. Management concern should be centered on the Company's overall strategy and its implementation in these general areas.

This paragraph is rather deceptive. It appears to be emphasizing the problem the writer feels is most important and suggesting the most important course of action to be followed. But if you read it closely, you will realize that it says very little. In extremely vague and general language, the writer directs the reader's attention to what looks like a major problem, but turns out to be little more than a conclusion that the company should be better managed. Example (11) was much better, although more subtle: It quietly emphasized the need for *gradual* growth.

Finally, a concluding paragraph should provide a sense of direction. It should indicate what the reader ought to be thinking about and what course of action it is most important for him to follow. In some respects, this third function is not too different from the second. Consider this example:

(14) The company's problems are many and complex, but related, and one cannot be satisfactorily solved without depending upon the solution of another. The present condition of the company and the intensity of competition imply that continuance of the present management policy will make survival of the company increasingly difficult.

What is the reader supposed to do now?

Here is an even more extreme case:

(15) As a whole, your company has more bad points than good points.

Example (11) did a fairly good job of indicating direction. Here is a more specific example:

(16) The purpose of this study was to investigate and make recommendations. Because little useful data were available, I have concentrated on identification of the information you need to control your operation. I have then attempted to show what analyses should be made with this information. The data are not easy to obtain and the analyses are not easy to make. Both require time and money. I feel the expenditure of both is necessary to maintain control over a rapidly expanding organization. I have tried to indicate exactly where and why money might be saved, and I believe the savings will more than offset the expenditures.

Notice how the writer has rounded out his report and given a sense of completeness. He has indicated clearly and specifically what he wishes to emphasize, and he has established, as specifically as he could within the limits of a single paragraph, just what the reader should do next. This is the kind of concluding paragraph that tells the reader that the writer knows what he is talking about.

10

GRAPHIC
PRESENTATION[1]

[1] This material on charts and graphs has been prepared by Kenneth W. Haemer of the American Telephone and Telegraph Company.

Graphic methods of presentation are an effective means of conveying information, and you should learn to use them where and when they are appropriate. The test to apply in deciding when to use charts and other graphs is simple: Ask yourself whether your reader will understand the information better or more easily if it is presented graphically.

Graphic presentation has three major virtues: It is concise, dramatic, and revealing. Graphs condense a large amount of information into a small space; when well designed they are forceful and convincing; and they can be extremely effective in explaining and clarifying the information you wish to convey.

There are three principal forms of graphic presentation that are effective for business reports: charts, maps, and diagrams. Charts answer the question "how much," maps show "where," and diagrams show "how."

In executive reports, graphic presentation usually consists of charts. Maps or diagrams are sometimes called for, but not often. Of course, a report concerned with how something is distributed geographically may use only map illustrations; a report discussing the organizational makeup of a company or the flow of money or goods might rely on diagrams. But in general the kind of information contained in reports can be conveyed best in chart form; for that reason, the following discussion of graphic presentation is centered on charts.

In most charts used in management and administrative reports the graphic part is geometrical rather than pictorial, making use of devices such as circles and bars and lines rather than pictures. One reason for this is that many important kinds of comparisons cannot be shown effectively in pictorial form. Another is that pictorial presentation is slower, more costly, and generally requires much more space for presenting a given amount of information. Nevertheless, pictorial charts have their place. They are valuable for their popular appeal, and are especially useful for presenting simple comparisons to audiences who are not familiar with conventional charts or who simply will not read them. Their field of use is in reports to customers, to employees, and to the general public; they are seldom appropriate in reports to management or administrative reports from management.

Charts used in business reports divide into two main groups: those using only one scale of measurement and those using two. (There are charts that make use of more than two scales, but they are specialized technical tools that are of no interest here.) In general, one-scale charts are much simpler and more limited than two-scale charts. However, you will find plenty of use for both types.

One-scale Charts

One-scale charts take two main forms: pie charts and bar charts.

A *pie chart* is a circle divided into wedge-shaped slices. Its purpose is to show how component parts add up to make a total. It is a good form for showing this sort of information because it so obviously adds up to 100 per cent, and it has the additional virtue of looking simple and nontechnical. Figure 10-1 is an effective use

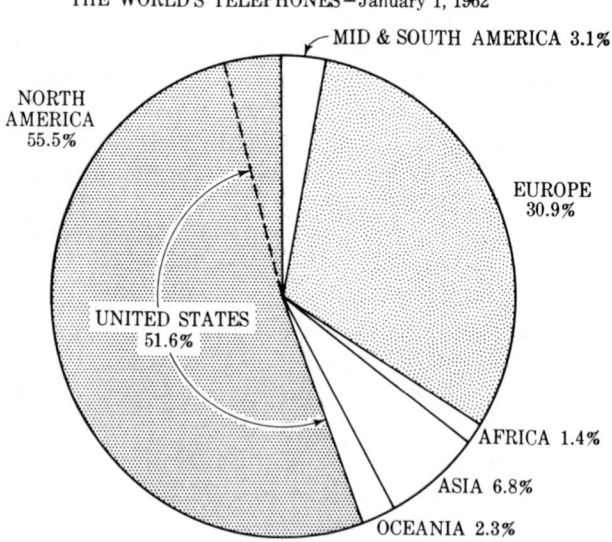

THE WORLD'S TELEPHONES – January 1, 1962

Figure 10-1 The pie chart shows the component parts that make up a total.

of this type of presentation: Notice particularly how the two parts of the major component are held together by using the same shading pattern for both.

But pie charts can be used for showing only the components that make up a whole. They are of little or no use for comparing changes from time to time or for comparing a series of totals of different size. In general, pie charts have a very limited usefulness and are awkward to handle. You will soon find that most of the amount comparisons you want to put into graphic form are not quite simple enough for a pie chart and that even when they are, another type of chart will usually do the job better.

Bar charts are made up of horizontal oblongs, placed one above the other. In this form of chart the length of each bar shows the size or amount of some item under study. Thus a bar chart is a means of comparing the magnitude of a series of items. In Figure 10-2, the portion of the labor force unemployed is quickly seen and compared for each of several Michigan cities.

PERCENT OF LABOR FORCE UNEMPLOYED–1955

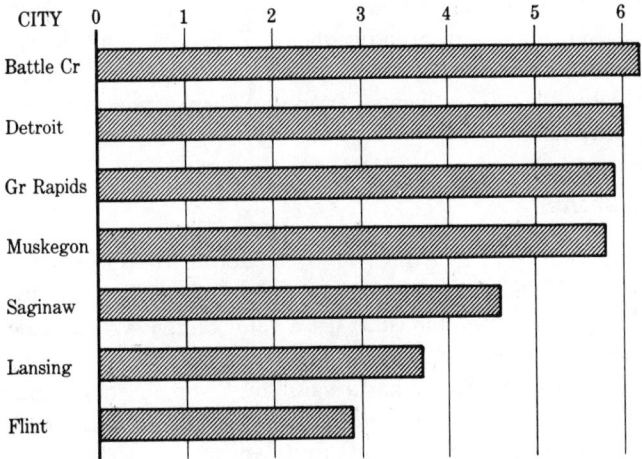

Figure 10-2 The simple bar chart compares *different things* at the *same time*.

Remember that this type of chart has only one scale and that it measures horizontally; the vertical dimension is used only to list the items. The order of items is flexible and may be varied in many useful ways. For example, items can be listed alphabetically, in order of size, importance, or in some arbitrary but established order such as men, women, children, or shareholders, employees, customers.

There are several subtypes of bar chart, each of which can be used to bring out a different aspect of the information under study.

As shown in Figure 10-3, the bars can be subdivided to show the component parts of each item. This chart provides the same information as a series of pie charts, but in a more manageable and compact form. Subdivided bars can be handled in two ways: The components of each bar can add up to a total amount in dollars, carloads, customers, or some other absolute measure, or they can add up to 100 per cent. In the 100 per cent form, the bars are, of course, all the same length and show the *proportion* of the total that each component part contributes.

Figures 10-4 and 10-5 show two other useful variations of a simple bar chart: Both are the result of adding a second set of information. The first goes by the name of *bar-and-symbol chart.* This is merely a simple bar chart with additional amounts showing such information as results for an earlier period, goals or standards, or results before or after some sort of adjustment. The other type brings two simple bar charts together for comparison. Shading the most important set of bars to set them off from the others makes this chart easier to understand.

Two-scale Charts

The identifying feature of this large family of charts is two scales placed at right angles; one measuring vertically, one horizontally. Thus each point drawn on the chart has a value on the vertical scale and a value on the horizontal, in the same way that the location of the New York Public Library has a value of 42 on the north and south (street) scale and a value of 5 on the east and west (avenue) scale. This two-scale arrangement permits you to picture all sorts of useful relationships that would be difficult to see in any other way.

Two-scale charts separate into three distinct yet related groups: line charts, surface charts, and column charts. Many of the varieties within each of these groups are matched by a corresponding variety in the other two groups. In fact, the same general kind of information can be shown in either line-chart, surface-chart, or column-chart form. However, these three forms aren't exact substitutes: As you will see, each provides a different emphasis, and usually one type is clearly more appropriate—for a specific set of data—than either of the others.

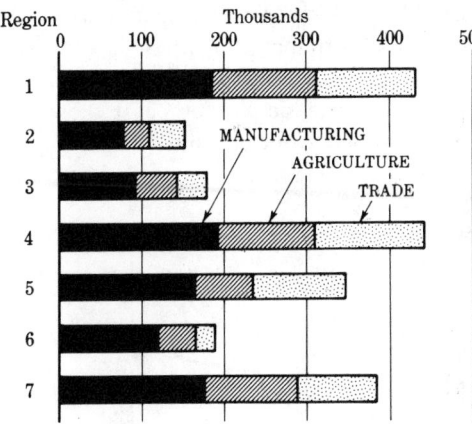

EMPLOYMENT – Major Occupational Groups

Figure 10-3 Subdivided bars show the component parts of several totals.

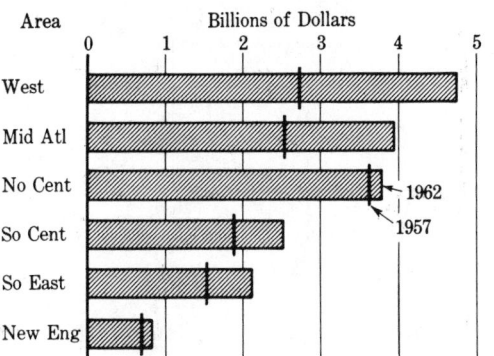

VALUE OF RESIDENTIAL CONSTRUCTION CONTRACTS

Figure 10-4 Bars and symbols compare results with earlier results.

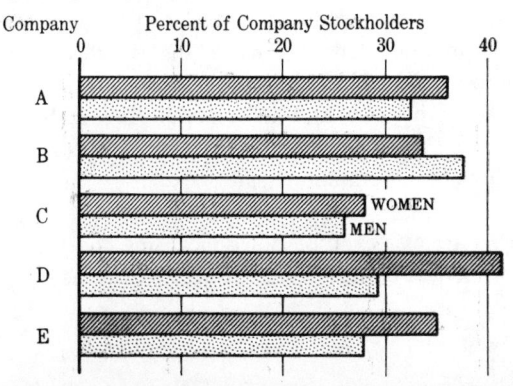

INDIVIDUALS OWNING STOCK
in 5 Large Corporations

Figure 10-5 Grouped bars compare two different but related sets of data.

A *line chart* is well described by its name. It is made by joining a series of points with a line. Although this line is called a *curve* in chart language, it may vary from extremely smooth to extremely jagged, depending on the behavior of the data presented.

The example below, Figure 10-6, is a simple line chart showing how the quantity of something varied from one time to the next.

ANNUAL PRODUCTION – ROCKET X14A2

Figure 10-6   The simple curve chart shows successive changes over a span of time.

It gives a clear, direct picture of how production dropped in the first few years and then increased rapidly, fell off again, then increased somewhat more slowly. In this type of chart—and most of the others that follow—the horizontal scale is used to measure *time,* the vertical scale to measure *number* or *quantity*.

Figure 10-7 is a somewhat more analytical chart: It shows a three-year span of data cut into yearly pieces and superimposed on a one-year chart. This form is especially useful for comparing each month this year with the same month in earlier years. It is widely used for such business data as production, sales, expenses, and earnings.

The next two illustrations are also examples of typical line charts. Figure 10-8 compares the behavior of three measures of business

MONTHLY OUTPUT–PLANT #7

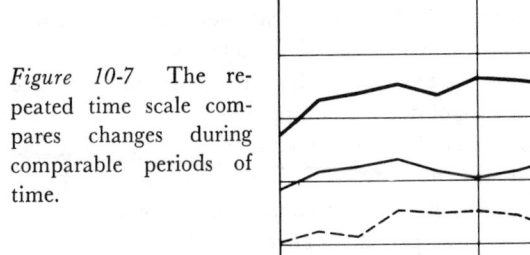

Figure 10-7 The re-
peated time scale com-
pares changes during
comparable periods of
time.

DECLINING INDUSTRIES
in a Growing Economy

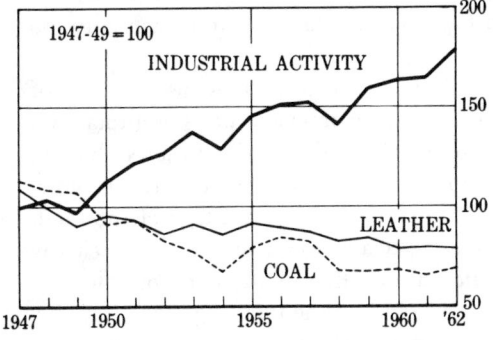

Figure 10-8 Multiple
curves compare changes
in two or more series of
data.

RADAR SET SC _ _ _ _

Figure 10-9 A combina-
tion of step curves and
slope curves compares
data that change
abruptly and those that
change gradually.

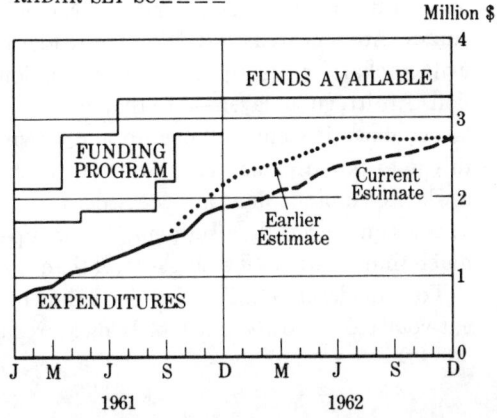

activity, showing clearly that the leather and coal industries are not following the pattern of industrial activity in general. The type of chart illustrated by Figure 10-9 is somewhat more complex, but is still clear and informative. This example is adapted from a chart used in the Department of Defense to show progress and plans for purchases of a certain type of defense equipment.

There are many other kinds of line charts, each useful for a specific purpose. In fact, this basic type of chart is so versatile that it is used more than any other in the internal administration and operation of all businesses, whether private or government.

A *surface chart* looks like a shaded line chart, and in its simplest form it is exactly that. If you shade a simple line chart between the curve and the base you get a simple surface chart; and the two are identical in meaning. The only difference is that the surface form is more striking. But shading other types of line chart changes their meaning. The reason is that in surface charts it is the distance *between* curves that is important; not the distance from each curve to the base.

The following examples illustrate the three most useful types of surface chart. The first two show the component parts of a total and how they change over a span of time. Figure 10-10 shows absolute amounts, such as dollars, tons, or employees; Figure 10-11 shows relative amounts, i.e., each component as a percentage of the total. The 100 per cent version is especially valuable because it clearly shows changes in the *relative* distribution of the parts of a total—changes that are easily overlooked when the total is growing rapidly.

Notice that in both cases the bottom layer is the only one that can be measured directly from the scale. The reader may, therefore, find it difficult to gauge the other layers with even approximate accuracy. Another weakness, from the reader's point of view, is that all surface charts are subject to an occupational disease—optical illusion. An irregular layer—one that moves up and down—makes all layers above it seem to move up and down also. The way to avoid this is to put irregular layers on top, if the order can be changed to do so. Another illusion occurs because a layer that moves along at the same level, then suddenly shoots up—or down—seems to be much thinner where it changes level than it really is.

To a moderate degree, the chart shown in Figure 10-12 lets you eat your cake and have it too. It measures the volume of "ins" and

EMPLOYEES – BY TERM OF SERVICE

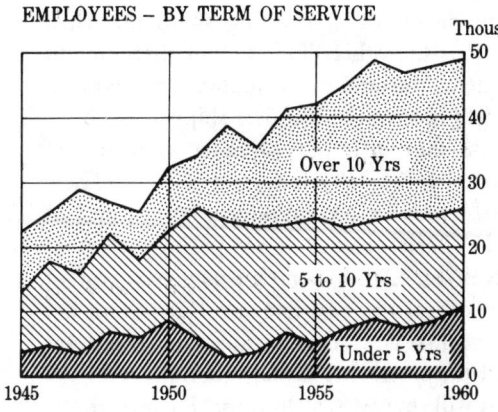

Figure 10-10 Subdivided surface shows the changes in the component parts of a total.

PERCENTAGE DISTRIBUTION OF EMPLOYEES
By Term of Service

Figure 10-11 The 100 per cent surface chart shows changes in the *relative* size of the components.

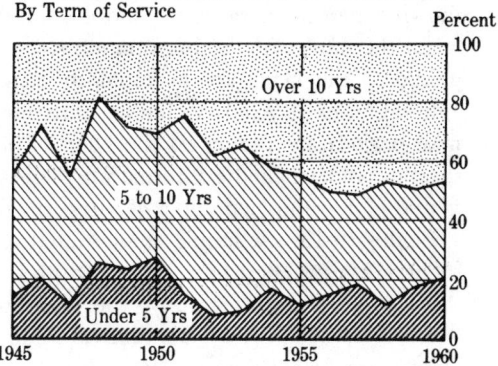

SALES ACTIVITY – Meton Corp.

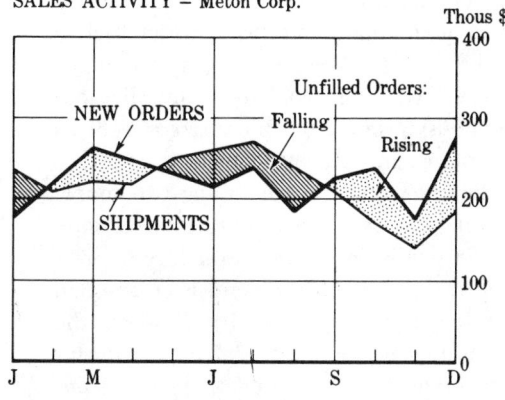

Figure 10-12 The income-outgo chart compares inward and outward movement, and emphasizes net differences.

"outs" and also shows, by means of contrasting shadings, when and by how much one exceeds the other. This sort of presentation is effective for picturing such information as imports and exports, revenues and expenses, orders received and orders shipped.

The next four illustrations show a family of charts that are related to line charts but look like bar charts turned on end. These charts, called *column charts,* provide an entirely different kind of comparison from that of bar charts. Instead of comparing a number of different items at a given time, they compare a given item at different times, in the same general way that line or surface charts do.

Column charts are, in fact, first cousins to surface charts and are useful for the same general purposes. But usually the nature of the information to be presented will suggest which to use. Surface charts are better when there are a large number of time periods to be shown, when the data do not move up and down very sharply, and when the nature of the information suggests a carry-over from one period to the next (for example, average number of acres under cultivation each year). Column charts are better when only a few time periods are shown on the chart, when the data change level sharply, and when the information suggests a fresh start for each period (for example, number of acres added each year).

Figure 10-13 is a simple column chart showing the money spent for new construction by a large and growing company. It tells the story directly and forcefully, the separated columns emphasizing the size of each year's expenditures. Figure 10-14 is the same kind of component-parts presentation that is used on the bar chart in Figure 10-3. Note that the columns are divided into four segments in this example. The use of more than four segments in such a chart is generally unwise, because the reader is given too many things to keep track of. Usually you can avoid too many divisions by combining some: either by using fewer but broader components or by lumping several small components under "all other."

The next two examples show the result of combining two simple column charts and of presenting differences instead of totals. Figure 10-15 presents a picture of gradually increasing farm income in a forceful way. You can easily see that this form is much better than a line chart would be for so few amounts. Figure 10-16 stresses the net gain or loss resulting from an "income" and an "outgo," in this case the difference between quantities put in and those taken out

EXPENDITURES FOR NEW CONSTRUCTION
West Coast Aluminum Corp.

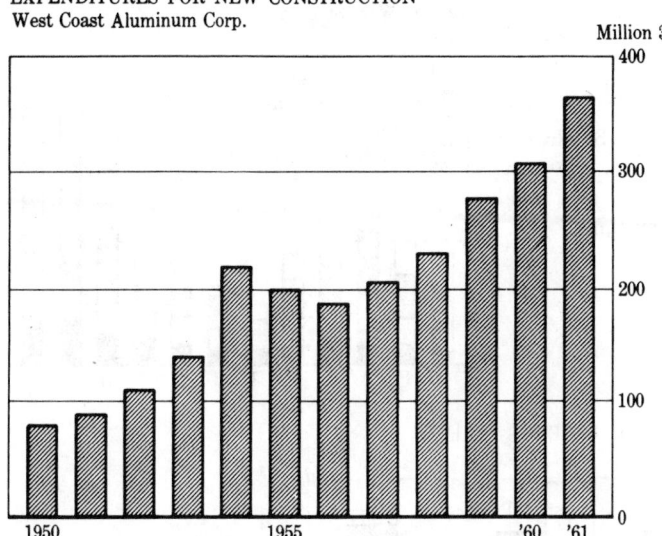

Figure 10-13 The simple column chart compares the *same things* at *different times.*

of stock. (Compare this closeup of net results with Figure 10-12, which measures the income and outgo but shows the differences only indirectly.)

There are other families of two-scale charts, but most of these are too technical for management reports. Only one needs to be mentioned here: the so-called frequency chart. Frequency charts use a different set of scales than time-series charts. Instead of amount, the vertical scale measures frequency of occurrence; instead of time, the horizontal scale classifies size. A chart showing the number of employees (frequency measure) in each of several wage groups (size measure) is a typical frequency chart. In appearance these charts take the form of simple curve or column charts.

As you can readily see, there is a wide variety of charts to choose from, each useful in its own way. Before deciding which kind to use, be sure you have a clear understanding of what the data mean and precisely what aspect of the data the picture is to focus on. No two types of chart serve exactly the same purpose, and so the type chosen should be the one that conveys information most clearly,

MAJOR ISSUES
Causing Work Stoppages

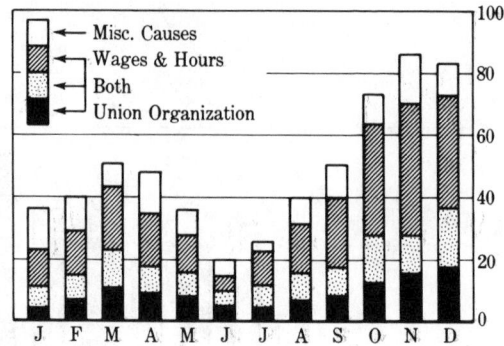

Figure 10-14 Subdivided columns show the component parts of a total at different times.

FARMERS' CASH RECEIPTS – Michigan

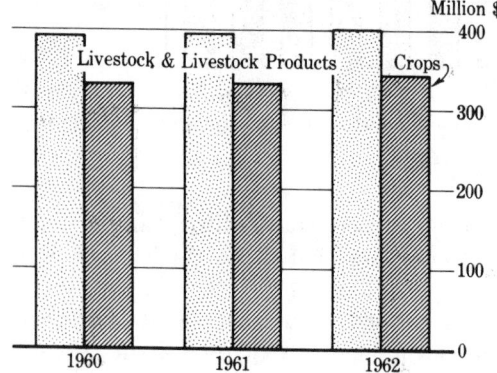

Figure 10-15 Grouped columns compare two related series of data over a span of time.

INVENTORY CHANGES – Selected Industries

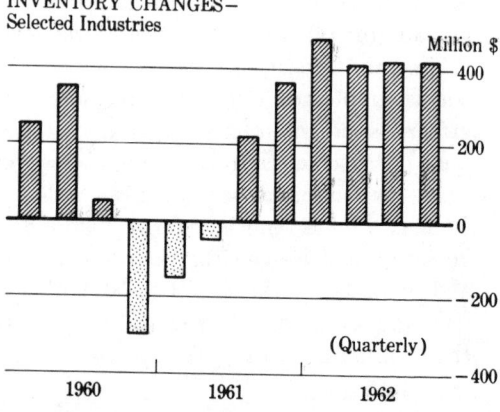

Figure 10-16 Net-gain-or-loss columns measure the differences between total income and outgo.

accurately, and forcefully. Be sure to avoid these two extremes: Don't rely on one or two favorite types regardless of whether they suit the purpose or not; don't invent types that are so special and complex that no one else will understand them.

In designing charts, the most important thing is the choice of scale. As shown by the examples in Figure 10-17, the same informa-

Figure 10-17 The importance of scale selection: the same data plotted on different amount scales.

tion can be scaled to give widely different impressions. There is no rule for proper scaling; the correct scale is the one that produces the appropriate effect. What is appropriate will depend on the purpose of the report, the subject matter, the circumstances under which it is being studied, and your estimate of how important the changes or differences really are. For example, a million-dollar increase in the national debt is scarcely worth mentioning; a million-dollar increase in a manufacturing company's debt is quite a different matter.

Although charts are valuable mainly because they are graphic, note that they are meaningless without words and figures to explain and measure. How these words and figures are handled is just as important as how the graphic part of the chart is designed. In general, the same principles that apply to clear, informative writing apply equally to chart titles, labels, and captions, but with even more force. A single inept, foggy, or long-winded sentence may escape notice, but a poor chart title will not.

Chart titling is especially important because of the growing use of statement, or "narrative," titles. Instead of merely identifying the subject matter of the chart, this type of title tells what the chart shows. Sometimes it even goes a step further and explains the causes behind the results or the conclusions they lead to. As you can see

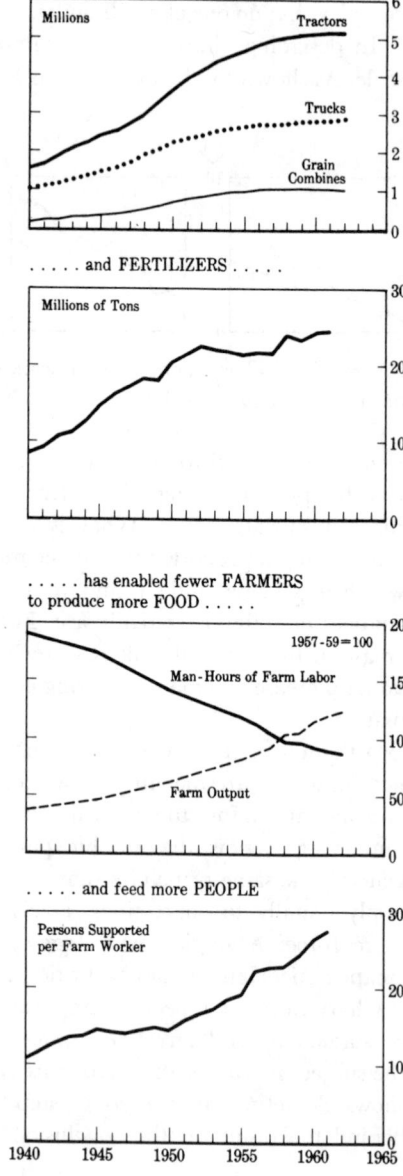

Increased use of MACHINES . . . . .

. . . . . and FERTILIZERS . . . . .

. . . . . has enabled fewer FARMERS
to produce more FOOD . . . . .

. . . . . and feed more PEOPLE

Figure 10-18 "Narrative" charts: related charts connected by titles that state the meaning of the data. This method of titling can be used also for single charts.

from the example in Figure 10-18, this method is effective. It helps the reader to understand the chart more quickly and to remember its message more easily.

Although graphic presentation is excellent when it is appropriate, there are several cautions about using it:

1. *Don't use so many charts that they overwhelm the rest of the report.* The reader will either ignore everything else, or—if he doesn't like charts—ignore the entire report.
2. *Use charts to explain or support the major points in the report.* The fewer charts you use, the more attention each gets; so if you use only one or two, it is doubly important that they relate to the main facts you are trying to convey.
3. *Don't try to convey too much information on one chart.* If you do, it will be cluttered and hard to understand. It's better to put the information in two simple charts than to crowd it into one complex one.
4. *Design the chart to focus on the meaning you are trying to convey.* Don't merely convert figures into graphic form and expect this to tell the reader what you want him to know.
5. *Keep the chart simple.* Leave out all unnecessary frills and trimmings. Don't add technical notes and other details that are not needed to *understand* the chart.
6. *Tie the chart in with your written presentation* by referring to it in the written text and by placing it as close as possible to the section of the text where you discuss it. This will spare your reader the annoyance of holding his thumb on page 4 when you refer him to a chart on page 45.

A CONCLUDING
WORD FROM
THE AUTHORS

The report-writing function of business will unquestionably increase in importance. As companies grow larger and employ more people, and as the complexities of business life mushroom, the number of reports required to maintain communication increases not in an arithmetical progression of 1, 2, 3, 4, but more nearly in a geometrical progression of 2, 4, 8, 16. Added to increasing corporate size is increasing physical distance, resulting from the trend toward widely separated plants and agencies and creating an attendant need for better communication through reports. Businessmen even estimate an employee's status in the organization by saying "He reports directly to the vice-president" or "He reports to the sales manager."

The ability to write effective reports is, therefore, one of the most useful skills you can acquire in your career in business. Often you will be judged solely on the basis of the reports you write, many times by key personnel who have no other contact with you. Whether you view a report-writing assignment as an opportunity or an ordeal will depend largely on how well you can learn the techniques of report writing, for we like to do the things we know we can do well. This is why most of the complaints about the need to write reports in business come from employees who can't write them effectively. Business badly needs people who can write clear, concise, accurate, readable reports, and if you can fill this need, you will go far. It is no exaggeration to say that in modern business a man is known by the quality of the reports he writes.

Your business career will unquestionably involve a myriad of reporting situations; you will write reports directly to one other person, reports to groups, reports that are passed up or down through several levels of authority, reports for other people to sign, reports written with other people, reports concisely digesting other reports, and other variations adapted to the particular demands of your firm. Here we repeat our admonition in the introduction to this book: Remember that you must have your reader always in mind. You must always be thinking of what *he* wants to learn, what you want *him* to learn, what reactions you want to produce in *him*. And the way you accomplish this demanding objective is both to learn the principles of good report writing and to apply them to the specific on-the-job situation which you encounter.

BIBLIOGRAPHY

There are hundreds of books and articles dealing with problems in communication, all of which are to some extent relevant to report writing. The following are suggested as particularly worthwhile for their relevance and their informative or provocative treatment of the subject:

JACQUES BARZUN AND HENRY F. GRAFF, *The Modern Researcher,* New York: Harcourt, Brace & World, Inc., 1957.
This book, now a paperback, discusses the organization and gathering of data as well as the presentation of research findings. It will be most useful for library research, not so helpful for field research.

MONROE C. BEARDSLEY, *Practical Logic,* Englewood Cliffs, N.J.: Prentice-Hall, Inc., 1950.
This little book, written by a professor of philosophy, is also available in a shorter textbook edition, same publisher and date, called *Thinking Straight.* While it does not even mention reports, it could be particularly useful to report writers, for the same processes of straight thinking presented in the book should lie behind all effective reports.

MARGARET D. BLICKLE AND MARTHA E. PASSE (EDS.), *Readings for Technical Writers,* New York: The Ronald Press Company, 1963.
An anthology of selected writings on the general problems of technical writing, the audience for technical material, and the organization and style of technical material.

M. JOSEPH DOOHER (ED.), *Effective Communication on the Job,* New York: American Management Association, 1956.

A collection of articles by 22 experts, covering all phases of business communication and subtitled "A Guide to Employee Communication for Supervisors and Executives."

HERMAN A. ESTRIN (ED.), *Technical and Professional Writing: A Practical Anthology,* New York: Harcourt, Brace & World, Inc., 1963.
Although the emphasis is primarily upon engineering and scientific writing, this collection offers advice of considerable value to business writers on the principles involved in attaining a clear and readable style.

ROBERT FERBER AND P. J. VERDOORN, *Research Methods in Economics and Business,* New York: The Macmillan Company, 1962.
This detailed research guide is oriented toward marketing but contains helpful advice on methodology for all fields of business research.

RUDOLPH FLESCH, *The Art of Readable Writing,* New York: Harper & Row, Publishers, Incorporated, 1949.
Here you will find an explanation of the Readability Formula (pages 213–216), along with sound common sense on writing. The book analyzes what kind of writing will fit what kind of audience and contains interesting examples which illustrate the general principles of readability.

HENRY WATSON FOWLER, *A Dictionary of Modern English Usage,* Oxford: Clarendon Press, 1953.
For readers with a sense of humor and a feeling for precision in language, this book, which has sold more than a half-million copies since 1926, is a *must.* It is a mixture of dictionary, style book, and arbiter of good taste in writing which has become a classic. It will not replace a desk dictionary, but for careful readers it will replace a lot of stereotyped writing. For Fowler at his best, look up "Battered Ornaments," "Elegant Variations," "Formal Words," "Hackneyed Phrases," "Love of the Long Word," and "Split Infinitives."

JOHN E. FREUND AND FRANK J. WILLIAMS, *Elementary Business Statistics,* Englewood Cliffs, N.J.: Prentice-Hall, Inc., 1964.
This is an introductory textbook on business statistics.

WILLIAM GILMAN, *The Language of Science,* New York: Harcourt, Brace & World, Inc., 1961.
This is a useful book for engineers and scientists.

SIR ERNEST GOWERS, *Plain Words: Their ABC,* New York: Alfred A. Knopf, Inc., 1954.
This book has been called a condensed and up-to-date version of Fowler's *A Dictionary of Modern English Usage.* Intended originally for the use of

British civil servants, it has had a far wider circulation because of its urbanity and wit. While many of the examples are taken from official writing in British government circles, the fundamental principles of communication and the emphasis on choice of words are excellent.

J. B. GREENOUGH AND G. L. KITTREDGE, *Words and Their Ways in English Speech,* Boston: Beacon Press, 1962.
This is an interesting book on word usage, a literary rather than a business guide.

ROBERT GUNNING, *The Technique of Clear Writing,* New York: McGraw-Hill Book Company, 1952.
This book has 10 chapters, each one devoted to a basic principle of clear, readable writing. It presents another yardstick to test readability, called the Fog Index, explained on pages 36–39.

DARREL HUFF, *How to Lie with Statistics,* New York: W. W. Norton & Company, Inc., 1954.
Much of this is written with tongue in cheek, but writers of reports can learn a great deal about "conclusions" drawn from statistics which do not add up to anything.

WILLARD V. MERRIHUE, *Managing by Communication,* New York: McGraw-Hill Book Company, 1960.
Although it is intended for executives, other readers may profit from this examination of the importance of the communication function as a tool of management.

M. J. MORONEY, *Facts from Figures,* Baltimore: Penguin Books, Inc., 3d and rev. ed., 1957.
This is a simply written and inexpensive book, dealing with statistics generally and including discussion of business statistics.

HERBERT C. MORTON, *Putting Words to Work,* Hanover, N.H.: Amos Tuck School of Business Administration, Dartmouth College, 1955.
This 12-page pamphlet, subtitled "What Business Has Learned about Writing," discusses the methods used by various companies to improve written communications.

ROBERT NEWCOMB AND MARG SAMMONS, *Employee Communications in Action,* New York: Harper & Row, Publishers, Incorporated, 1961.
An interesting study of the role of communication in the relationship between management and labor.

ALEX F. OSBORN, *Applied Imagination, Principles and Procedures of Creative Thinking,* New York: Charles Scribner's Sons, 1953.

An important book, relevant to the current debate in business and educational circles on whether creativity can be learned and taught. Mr. Osborn thinks it can be, and since creative thinking lies at the roots of good writing, this is a challenging book for anyone interested in communication even though business writing is not its subject.

CHARLES E. REDFIELD, *Communication in Management,* Chicago: The University of Chicago Press, 1953.

A general treatment of management's problems and methods of communication as information goes down, up, and horizontally. The bibliographies at the ends of chapters and the comprehensive bibliography at the end of the book are invaluable guides to those who want additional articles and books on all phases of communication in business.

ROBERT SCHLAIFER, *Introduction to Statistics for Business Decisions,* New York: McGraw-Hill Book Company, 1961.

This is an introductory textbook dealing with Bayesian statistics and their use in business.

ROBERT SCHLAIFER, *Probability and Statistics for Business Decisions,* New York: McGraw-Hill Book Company, 1959.

This is a more difficult book than the preceding, covering a wider range of topics.

NORMAN G. SHIDLE, *Clear Writing for Easy Reading,* New York: McGraw-Hill Book Company, 1951.

A brief practical approach to the problems of writing, with numerous specific suggestions for eliminating wordiness and other common faults.

ROBERT L. SHURTER AND J. PETER WILLIAMSON, *Written Communication in Business,* New York: McGraw-Hill Book Company, 2d ed., 1964.

This is a college text designed for undergraduate and graduate students and includes problems and cases.

WILLARD STRUNK, JR., *The Elements of Style,* revised by E. B. White, New York: The Macmillan Company, 1959.

This concise and convenient handbook is a modern classic because of its common-sense treatment of the basic principles of writing and the requirements for a clear and readable style.

W. A. WALLIS AND H. V. ROBERTS, *Statistics: A New Approach,* New York, The Free Press of Glencoe, 1956.

This is a basic statistics textbook, particularly useful for business statistics.

FRANCIS W. WEEKS (ED.), *Readings in Communication from Fortune,* New York: Holt, Rinehart and Winston, Inc., 1961.

A useful collection of 28 articles from *Fortune* which deal with the methods, content, and effects of communication in the modern business world by such well-known writers as William H. Whyte, Jr., Perrin Stryker, Bernard De Voto, Daniel Seligman, and others.

WILLIAM H. WHYTE, JR., AND THE EDITORS OF FORTUNE, *Is Anybody Listening?* New York: Simon and Schuster, Inc., 1952.
Based on a series of articles which originally appeared in *Fortune,* this is a penetrating and provocative analysis of how and why business fumbles its communications. The chapters on "The Language of Business" and "The Prose Engineers" are particularly good.

The following are also useful references:

LAWRENCE D. BRENNAN, *Business Communication,* Paterson, N.J.: Littlefield, Adams & Co., 1960.

LELAND BROWN, *Communicating Facts and Ideas in Business,* Englewood Cliffs, N.J.: Prentice-Hall, Inc., 1961.

DAVID B. COMER AND RALPH SPILLMAN, *Modern Technical and Industrial Reports,* New York: G. P. Putnam's Sons, 1962.

CARL G. GAUM, H. F. GRAVES, AND L. S. S. HOFFMAN, *Report Writing,* Englewood Cliffs, N.J.: Prentice-Hall, Inc., 1950.

WILLIAM C. HIMSTREET AND WAYNE M. BATY, *Business Communications: Principles and Methods,* San Francisco: Wadsworth Publishing Company, Inc., 1961.

J. N. HOOK, *Hook's Guide to Good Writing,* New York: The Ronald Press Company, 1962.

F. KEREKES AND R. WINFREY, *Report Preparation,* Ames, Iowa: The Iowa State University Press, 1951.

RAYMOND V. LESIKAR, *Report Writing for Business,* Homewood, Ill.: Richard D. Irwin, Inc., 1961.

CALVIN D. LINTON, *How to Write Reports,* New York: Harper & Row, Publishers, Incorporated, 1954.

DONALD H. MENZEL, HOWARD MUMFORD JONES, AND LYLE G. BOYD, *Writing a Technical Paper,* New York: McGraw-Hill Book Company, 1961.

G. H. MILLS AND J. A. WALTER, *Technical Writing,* New York: Holt, Rinehart and Winston, Inc., 1954.

NORMAN B. SIGBAND, *Effective Report Writing,* New York: Harper & Row, Publishers, Incorporated, 1960.

ARNOLD B. SKLARE, *Creative Report Writing,* New York: McGraw-Hill Book Company, 1964.

ROBERT E. TUTTLE AND C. A. BROWN, *Writing Useful Reports,* New York: Appleton-Century-Crofts, Inc., 1956.

JOSEPH N. ULMAN, JR., *Technical Reporting,* New York: Holt, Rinehart and Winston, Inc., 1952.

INDEX